===== Praise for Paul Ferrini's Books =====

"The most important book I have read. I study it like a bible!" Elisabeth Kubler-Ross, M.D., author of *On Death and Dying*.

"These words embody tolerance, universality, love and compassion—hallmarks of all Great Teachings. They turn our attention inward to our own divine nature, instead of diverting it outward. Paul Ferrini is a modern-day Kahlil Gibran—poet, mystic, visionary, teller of truth." Larry Dossey, M.D., author of *Healing Words: The Power of Prayer and the Practice of Medicine*.

"Paul Ferrini leads us skillfully and courageously beyond shame, blame and attachment to our wounds into the depths of self-forgiveness. His work is a must-read for all people who are ready to take responsibility for their own healing." John Bradshaw, author of *Family Secrets*.

"A breath of fresh air in an often musty and cluttered domain. With sweetness, clarity, and simplicity we are directed to the truth within. I read this book whenever my heart directs, which is often." Pat Rodegast, author of *Emmanuel's Book I, II and III*.

"Paul Ferrini's writing is authentic, delightful and wise. It reconnects the reader to the Spirit Within, to that place where even our deepest wounds can be healed." Joan Borysenko, Ph.D., author of *Guilt is the Teacher, Love is the Answer*.

"I feel that this work comes from a continuous friendship with the deepest part of the Self. I trust its wisdom." Coleman Barks, poet and translator.

"Paul Ferrini's wonderful books show a way to walk lightly with joy on planet earth." Gerald Jampolsky, M.D., author of *Love is Letting Go of Fear*.

"Paul Ferrini leads us on a gentle journey to our true source of joy and happiness—inside ourselves." Ken Keyes, Jr., author of *The Handbook of Higher Consciousness*.

Book Design by Paul Ferrini
Typesetting by Ruth Todrin

Artwork on front and back cover by Andrée Clearwater. Photograph on page 6 and back cover by Barbara McAlley through Carol Bruce and Robert Ferre. Photograph on page 40 of painting by Heinrich Hoffman. Drawing on page 126 by Teddy Swecker. Drawing on page 196 of D.T. Suzuki by Margaret Holt.

For my three teachers:
Lao Tzu, Martin Buber, Jesus of Nazareth

with special thanks to my daughter Shanti
who helped hold the space
in which this book was born

ISBN # 1-879159-16-3

Manufactured in the United States of America

The Silence of the Heart

of the

Heart

Reflections of the Christ Mind
Part Two

Paul Ferrini

Table of Contents

The Silence
of the Heart

Silence is the essence of the heart. You cannot be in the heart unless you are in forgiveness of yourself and others. You cannot be in the heart if you are worried or angry. You cannot be in the heart if your breathing is shallow or labored.

When the breath is shallow, thinking is superficial. If you want to live a spiritual life, bring your awareness to your breath. Become aware of the times when you are breathing in a shallow way and bring your awareness to your thoughts. You will see that your mind is chattering. None of these thoughts has depth or significance. If you relax and breathe deeply, these thoughts will fly away like startled birds. And then you will abide in the heart

When the breath is labored, thinking is driven by fear and anxiety. Become aware when your breathing is labored. Notice what you are thinking and feeling. Your mindstates will be rooted in the past or future. You will be focused on what other people are doing and how you can accommodate them or protect yourself from their actions. You are building a fortress of thought around your heart. Take a deep breath and relax. Now take another one. Breathe and return to the heart. Breathe and return to your essential Self.

Unless you return to the heart, you cannot see with compassion. And one who does not see with compassion does not see accurately. All that is perceived is a fabrication, a hyperbole. It simply feeds your boredom or anxiety.

Breathing is the key to living a spiritual life in physical embodiment. When the body dies, the breath leaves the body. Where does it go?

Most of you think that the body is the creator of the breath. Actually, it is the other way around. The breath is the begetter of the body. When the breath goes, the body ceases to function. It disintegrates into nothing because, without the breath of spirit, the body is nothing.

If you want to lead a spiritual life breathe deeply and slowly. Take the air deep down into your abdomen and release it fully. The more air you bring into your body, the lighter it will feel, and the easier it will be for you to accomplish your responsibilities. One who breathes is not afraid or overwhelmed by what life presents because he or she has the energy to meet all circumstances. Only one whose breathing is shallow or labored and irregular is de-energized and easily intimidated by the challenges of life.

Unless you breathe deeply and calmly, you cannot be in your heart. If you do not know what I am talking about, put this book down and begin to breathe into your abdomen, counting to five on the inhalation and counting again to five on the exhalation. Breathe in this way for five minutes, gradually extending your count to seven, or eight, or nine. Do not force. Just expand gradually, as your lungs comfortably allow.

Now you are in your heart. Notice that you are deeply relaxed, yet surprisingly alert. Your consciousness extends to all the cells of your body. You are content where you are. You fully inhabit your body in the present moment. You feel warm and energetic. You feel safe and secure. Your thoughts have slowed down and become more integral. You are no longer focusing on the "shoulds" and "what ifs" of your life. Tension and anxiety are absent. Past and future have receded from your awareness. Your thinking is centered and dignified. You can stay with your thoughts because they are fewer and further between. Now bring your awareness to your heart, as you continue to breathe gently but deeply into your abdomen.

Can you feel the presence of understanding and compassion in your heart center? Can you see that you hold yourself and others in gentle acceptance? Can you feel the love that dwells in your heart and freely extends to others?

Now you are in your heart. Now you are in the silence from which all sound comes. Like a boat on the ocean you feel the waves swell beneath you. And you move with the waves, yet you know you are not the waves. Thoughts come and go, yet you know you are not the thoughts. Some thoughts propel you further out than others, yet still you can return to your center. Like a large wave, a particular thought may be charged with emotion, yet if you remain where you are, the emotion will subside. Now you know you can abide the ebb and flow of the tide, moving out and moving in, feeling the contraction and expansion of thought.

Beneath the thinking mind is a pure, non-judgmental awareness. As soon as you discover that awareness, the heart opens, and giving and receiving are effortless.

Observing silence, and breathing deeply and gently is the easiest way to open the heart. You can also open it through sacred dancing and movements which incorporate the breath and encourage gratitude and presence in the moment. The method you use to fall into the heart is just a tool. Do not make it important. What is important is that you find a way to access the deeper aspect of your being which is at peace.

There is no human being who is incapable of reaching this state of open awareness and compassion. However, very few people know that this capacity for peace exists in them. Most human beings live a fast pace life in which they struggle to make ends meet. Their minds are consumed with thinking, planning, and worrying. Their bodies are constantly in fight or flight, weakening the immune system and creating the conditions in which dis-ease can take hold.

Few human beings take direct responsibility for their physical and emotional well-being. It is no wonder that they lack a spiritual perspective on life. When people do not care for themselves, they blame others for their problems. They feel like victims. They feel trapped in their jobs, their relationships, their physical location, their roles and responsibilities. They appear to live inside a pressure cooker. Either they stay in their external situation and feel victimized and resentful. Or they leave that situation inappropriately before it is healed, leaving a wake of broken hearts.

If any of this sounds familiar, then you know only too

well how easy it is to get caught in the struggle of existence. Your life has speeded up—you are busier than ever before—but to what avail? Your money and possessions cannot buy you peace. Your name, fame and status in society cannot bring you happiness. Be honest with yourself. Do you feel good about yourself and the people closest to you? Are you optimistic about life? Do you look forward to each day? If not, you are living a life empty of spiritual nourishment, a life that has lost its rootedness in the breath, the body and the earth.

Speeding up life does not make it better. Traveling across the planet in cars and planes does not create closer relationships. Many of you feel that your lives are speeding up, but you do not realize that you are the one pouring the gas in the tank. I suppose it is easier for you to believe in the destruction of the planet through earthquakes and floods than to take responsibility for your desecration of the planet through your own anxiety, boredom, and carelessness.

Don't you see that the earth is simply reflecting back to you the quality of your own consciousness? Its pollution is none other than the pollution of your own heart-mind. The more you turn away from yourself, the more you abuse the earth and each other. The more you forget to breathe, the unhealthier the air gets, and the more interpersonal conflicts arise.

If you keep forgetting to breathe, the planet is doomed. "Well, " you say, "I can handle that." But it may not be as easy as you think. Try it for a while. Breathe deeply for one day and see what happens. If you are committed to this practice, all that is artificial in your life will begin to fall away. And you may be surprised how much of your life begins to unpeel.

Consider this. Is your job safe? Not if you go to work out of sacrifice. What about your marriage? Are you with your partner out of duty or love? What about your values and religious beliefs...are they safe? Or have they been fashioned out of guilt and fear? If so, they will not stand the ebb and flow as the breath comes down into the belly and out through the mouth, the nose, and the skin.

Do you really want to de-toxify? Do you really want to slow down? Are you ready to let the excess stimulation go?

"But," you ask, "can't I still read my paper and watch the news on TV? "

"Yes," I will tell you, "but only if you can keep breathing deeply and gently."

Most of you will find that this is impossible. To seek your peace means for the moment that you must forgo false stimulation in your life. Anything that is trivial or overly labored takes you away from the essence of who you are.

Don't ask me to spell everything out. I'm not going to give you a new set of commandments. Use your common sense. See what brings you peace and what disturbs your peace. Take responsibility for what you consume, who you are with, what you do. You have choices in life. One set of choices brings you struggle and pain. The other brings you quietude and healing.

Can you live without overstimulation? Can you slow down, breathe and live in the moment? It may not be as difficult as you think. Since you can only begin now, not in the past or future, it is a simple challenge. Try it now. Be in the present and breathe for a few minutes. The more you do it, the easier it will become. This practice will gather momentum, like a stream coming down from a mountain, taking with it all the blocks that stand in its way.

When you commit to the practice of silence, your relationship to the entire universe changes. Your communication deepens and extends. Those who know you understand without your telling them. Your meaning is carried by the breath and by the wind. There is no more difference between inner and outer. Earth and heaven meet where your heart and mind join in silent bliss.

Only your fear keeps you in resistance to life. Move through the fear by breathing and the resistance dissolves. Now you are flowing with the current of life. Do you need to get a job, be married, have children, write books, give talks, feed the hungry, save the disenfranchised and disheartened? Not unless they join you in the river. And if they do, you can be sure it is not you working, marrying, procreating, writing, talking, feeding or saving. It is the river doing it through you. And so you remain cheerful and at ease whatever you are doing. Nothing keeps you from breathing, because breathing is your only responsibility.

So I'll give you a very simple yardstick: "If you can't breathe, don't do it. And if you try to do it anyway, remember to breathe!"

For many years you have been moving too fast for the river to catch up to you. No wonder you don't feel supported by the universe! But, take heart, every indigenous people who have lived on the planet have known and practiced what I am teaching to you. And somewhere, deep in your heart, you know and remember it too. For once, before your ego tried to take charge of the journey, you were the patient captain of your own ship, moving without oars or sails to a destination intuited but unknown. And it is the same now, even though you think you must work at being in charge.

Breathe and in time the river of life will find you and adopt you. And then you will be its spokesman and its confidant. The one who listens and the one who tells the truth. The one who serves without saving.

And loves without asking in return.

All this is your destiny. To be the creator and the created, all in one. To be the male in the female and female in male. To be active and receptive. To go beyond duality on the wings of paradox.

All this you will do, because the Messiah has come and the Messiah is you. You are the one who learns to breathe the body and lift yourself out of the pain of self-created conflicts. You are the one, dear brother or sister. Only you.

Part 1

Integrity

Opening the Prison Door

Integrity is defined as the "quality or state of being complete or undivided." While clearly we aspire to have integrity, many of us do not feel either complete or undivided. We feel discouraged when we look within and our search for happiness with others exacerbates our deepest wounds.

There are no magical fixes for this condition. It is the raw material of life which has been given to us to transform. We must mold it and craft it into a work of art. That is what our life is: an opportunity to create ourselves.

It would be easy for the potter to reject the clay as inferior and unworthy of him. But were he to do so, his life would have no meaning. He is not defined by the clay, but by what he chooses to do with it.

What do we choose to do with the hand we have been dealt? How can we work with the challenges life has provided us to come to peace in our hearts and in our relationships?

The answer is a simple one, but it may not be the one you expect. The answer is that you don't have to do anything.

"Well," you ask, "how does the clay get molded if we don't have to do anything?"

The clay gets molded by our willingness to stay with and in our process. In our struggle, and in our surrender, the clay gets molded. The work of art is offered, torn apart, and offered once again. At some point, we know it is finished and we can work on it no more.

And then we walk away from it. Then, before we realize it, more clay is given into our hands. It has a different consistency, a different potential. It brings new challenges.

We do not have to mold the clay. Just being in our life is the molding process. Even when it seems that we are resisting our lives or denying what is happening, the clay is still being worked.

In other words, you can't be alive and not be engaged in creating a work of art.

"What about the criminal," you ask. "Has he created a work of art with his life?"

Yes, he has. His life is the record of his journey through his fears, just as your life is your record. Each of you has told your story. If you look into his heart, you will see that his story is not that different from your own.

There are no failures on this planet. Even the homeless, the prostitutes, the drug dealers, are molding the clay that was given to them.

Because you do not like a particular piece of artwork does not mean that it ceases to be a work of art. There are no boring stories out there. Each tale is a gem. Each sculpture has genius.

Integrity is a universal gift. Everyone has it. It is part of the clay itself. Whatever you build with your life will stand up. It will be there for you to reflect on and for others to see.

You may choose to leave it standing or to tear it down. That is your choice. Others may gawk and say unkind things. That is their choice. None of it means anything.

There is no right and wrong in this process. If there were, those of you who are "right" would be wearing permanent halos.

You cannot say that what one person builds with his life is less valuable than what another person builds. All you can say in truth is that you prefer what one person has built to what another has built. You have your preferences.

Fortunately God does not share them. Not yours or anyone else's. God listens to everyone's story. His ear is to each person's heart. Nobody has pushed Him away by making a mistake. All He ever wants to know is: "Did you learn from your mistake?"

Integrity is not something we have to earn. It is essential to who we are. There is no one here who does not have integrity, just as there is no one here who does not deserve love.

Of course, there are plenty of people who don't think they have integrity. And they have the unfortunate habit of trying to find their wholeness by demanding the time, attention, or possessions of others. These people are not evil. They are just confused. They don't know that their life is a work of art. They don't know that they are master sculptors. They think that they got a lousy hand.

One day they will realize that they got the perfect hand. And then they will start to work with it consciously and energetically. Until then, they are playing at being victims. They are playing at being broken, unhealed, unwhole.

A black person confined to a wheel chair may not feel whole, but he has no less integrity than anyone else. He has not been given inferior clay. There are no accidents in this life. Nobody got anybody else's clay.

You see the problem is not existential. Integrity is there in each one of us. The problem is that we believe we are not whole. We believe that we need to be fixed or that we can fix someone else. We feel a false sense of responsibility for others and we do not take enough responsibility for ourselves. We are driven by desire, greed, guilt and fear. We attack, defend, and then try to repair the damage. Of course, it doesn't work. The one who perceives the damage cannot fix it.

In truth, nothing is broken and nothing needs to be fixed. If we could dwell in this awareness, all our wounds would heal by themselves. Miracles would happen, because the ego structure blocking the miracle would dissolve.

This human drama seems to be about abuse, but it is really about learning to take responsibility. All suffering is a temporary construction created for your learning. And all the tools that you need to end your suffering have been given into your hands.

When we are not blaming each other for our problems, we are blaming God. We think it's His fault that we are unhappy. It's always someone else's fault why we aren't happy. We don't like being put to the test. Neither did Job.

It's not fun to have your magical beliefs crashed.

But we all need to realize that no magical incantation is going to open the door to the prison. It doesn't work that way. Freedom is much more simple and close at hand.

"Well," you say, "If I only had a helicopter or a 747 I could get out of this hole!" You don't realize how absurd that sounds.

Forget about that 747, brother. Just use the ladder.

"That old cruddy thing?" That can't possibly get me out of here!"

We all know the dialogue. We've had this conversation before.

Others keep pointing to the ladder, but we keep looking away. We have a certain attachment to being "innocent victims."

The problem is that the innocent victim will never acknowledge the ladder. He will never admit that he has the tools he needs to extricate himself from his suffering. For, as soon as he admits that he has these tools, he ceases to be a victim. Nobody feels sorry for him anymore. The game of being a handicapped creator comes to an end.

God keeps saying "I hate to tell you folks but there are no handicapped creators."

So if we want to discover our integrity we need to stop pretending to be victims. We need to stop pretending that we weren't given the right tools. We need to take the clay and work with it.

Anyone who does this stops complaining and gets on with his life. He learns to take care of himself and he gives others the space to take care of themselves. Indeed, he releases all sense of obligation to and from others so that he is free to follow the promptings of his mind and heart.

For the person who knows that wholeness has not been denied him, there are no excuses. There can be no procrastination. There is nothing that stands between him and his joy.

His life is his work of art and he is busy about it even as

a bee is busy pollinating flowers. If you speak to him of sacrifice, he will laugh and say: "work that is not joyful accomplishes nothing of value in the world." And, of course, he will be right.

One artist does not work for another unless he is learning something of value to his craft. When he stops learning, he moves to another teacher, or begins working on his own. Nobody can keep him from his craft. No one can take him out of his life. For his life and his craft are one.

In a world where everyone is a genius, there are no bosses and no employees. There are only teachers and students in voluntary association.

If you do not like where you are, you must leave that place or you do not honor yourself. Do not force yourself to stay in any environment in which you cease to remember that you are a creator of your life.

As I said, "leave your nets." Do not struggle to be worthy when you already are. Leave that job or relationship in which you are unable to remember who you are. Let go of your neurotic bargain for love and acceptance. And walk through your fears. You will never find your wings until you learn to use your arms and your legs. Don't ask God to do for you what you must learn to do for yourself.

In honoring yourself, you needn't make anyone else wrong. Just do what is good for you and express your gratitude to others. When you are stepping into your life, you do not leave others hastily or in anger. You say your goodbyes. You bless the person whose life you have shared and the place where you have lived. Because you can bless the past, you are free to leave it.

You cannot "leave your nets" and take the fish with you. In time, the fish will rot and leave a terrible stench. For miles around, people will anticipate your arrival. "The Fisherman is coming." Your past walks in front of you. This is not the way to freedom.

Throw the fish away. Give them their freedom so that you can claim your own.

Be strong in your conviction about your own life, but gentle with others. Do not judge their needs just because you cannot meet them. Just be honest about what you can and cannot do, and wish them well.

Remember, the one whom you reject follows you. Only acceptance brings completion.

When you are ready to leave the entanglements of your life and step out on the simple path of love and forgiveness, you will know it in your heart and mind. There will be no struggle, no deliberation.

In your clarity and generosity, others will relax and release you. And you will hold them in your heart wherever you go.

The only prisons in the world are the ones of your own making. And only one who is ignorant of his own genius could hold another hostage against his will.

Remember, dear brother and sister: for every prison you create in your mind, there is a key that unlocks the door. If you can't erase the prison, at least claim the key to the door.

You are not a victim of the world, but the one who holds the key to freedom. In your eyes is the spark of divine light that leads all beings out of the darkness of fear and mistrust. And in your heart is the love that gives birth to all the myriad beings in the universe. Your essence is unbroken, whole, dynamic and creative. It but awaits your trust.

The Futility of Control

The key to living in peace is the ability to stay in the present moment. You cannot live in the present moment if you think you are the one "doing" your life.

If you think you are the "doer," you will feel justified in making endless plans. Now, I do not suggest that you try to stop making plans. I ask you instead to watch carefully what happens to your plans. See how they inevitably change, reverse themselves, or even dissolve into thin air as you begin to live out your experience. No matter how hard you try to pin your life down, there are inevitable surprises. And you should be grateful for them. Without these surprises, your existence would be one-dimensional, routine and boring.

Your ego is terrified of the unknown. No matter how terrible the known past is, the ego prefers it to the unknown present. All of its energy goes into trying to make the present into the past. It thinks that this creates safety, but in truth it creates continued terror, a constant aggravation of the wound until the pain is so intense that it must be dealt with. You see, everything, even your ego, conspires toward your awakening!

So living the past over and over again creates the ultimate terror. Outwardly, life seems safe and predictable. Inwardly, the dynamite has been lit.

You think you are the doer of your life and that you have created safety, when in fact your life is about to explode and you are about to realize that you have no conscious control over what happens. You believe that you are powerful, yet you demonstrate again and again your utter powerlessness.

This is an interesting paradox, is it not? No matter how hard it tries, the ego cannot create safety. No matter how many times the ego tries to push you out of the present moment, it inevitably brings you into it full force, because the price of denial is pain.

The more you seek to control life the more life will give you the message that it cannot be controlled. And then you will feel powerless and try even harder to control. You see? It is a silly game. You cannot win the game, yet you can't stop playing it either. This is the one supreme addiction. It has many forms. Even the attachment to risk-taking is a form of control. The forms are endless.

When you begin to realize that you are not the doer, you drop the subconscious attachment to playing to lose. As a result, you are no longer the victim of your life. When you cease being the doer, you also cease being the victim, for the two always go hand in hand. The doer is the victim and the victim the doer. This is the cycle of birth and death, the karmic wheel on which you have been mercilessly turning.

When the wheel stops turning, you enter the unknown courageously, without bringing the past, without projecting the future. You learn to face your fears of the unknown directly. And, as you do, you discover the gifts and miracles that lie on the other side of your fear.

The price of the miracle is not great. You must simply give up what you think you know. When the past drops and all of your knowledge comes to an end, your innocence is restored. You enter the moment fully conscious, allowing it to unfold in you and through you. This is not some idle fantasy, but an invitation to experience, an invitation to participate in the ongoing miracle of life.

Three Stages of Consciousness

There are three stages in the development of human consciousness. The first stage is Subconscious Knowledge. Driven by instinct and emotions, this is the state of ancient man, or man as animal. The second stage is Conscious Knowledge. It is characterized by the quest for information, which builds the intellect but ultimately comes up spiritually empty. This is the state of modern man, or man as thinker. The third stage is Super-Conscious Knowledge. It is the state of total surrender of all intellectual solutions, all need to control or plan. It is characterized by conscious unknowing. It is the the state of the divine person, or co-creator. You are living at a time when stage two is coming to closure and stage three is being born.

The entrance into stage three calls for a different way of living individually and collectively. It calls for a repudiation of the controlling mind. It calls for a thorough investigation of that mind, the fears on which it is based, and the utter futility of its creations.

Living in fear, the ego-mind seeks safety, but never finds it. Because it never investigates its own fear, it is constantly driven by that fear unconsciously, and its creations are unconscious projections of that fear. This includes all its relationship dramas.

Fear must be faced. It must be dealt with. It must be made conscious. This brings the darkness to the light. It ends the split between ego and spirit, inner and outer. The light that comes when darkness has been fully explored is not the same light that was there when darkness was pushed away. In stage one, you reject the darkness because you are afraid of it. In stage two, you push it away by trying to explain it. And in stage three, you embrace the darkness and integrate it.

In stage two, your joy was thin and capable of cracking. Any deep challenge would undermine it. In stage three, your joy is fathoms deep. Challenges are accepted and perfected in it. There is no place in a joy this deep for even the possibility of punishment. This is not the joy of Adam in the garden. But the joy of Job in the desert.

Stage three is all about undoing the conceit of the ego mind. In stage one, man is ignorant of God. The Old Testament is the teaching for stage one man. It stays: "Do this or God will punish you!" It is fear-based at the deepest emotional level. That is why God destroys whole cities in his wrath. The message to man is "become aware of God outside of you."

In stage two, man is aware of God but still separate from him. The New Testament is the teaching for stage two man. It says: "God is not vengeful. He loves you and asks you to come and embrace his teaching. Your life will be happier if you make room for God in your life." Stage two teachings focus on what you will miss if you keep God out of your life. It is the teaching of persuasion, still based on fear and separation.

My teaching was always a stage three teaching. I have always said to you: "you will find God in your own heart and in the hearts of your brothers. God cannot ever be separate from you, for the divine is your very essence." But when the stage three teaching is heard by stage two ears, the result is a stage two interpretation of that teaching.

Now this is changing. Many of you are hearing the teaching as it was originally intended. You are in communion with me in your daily lives. You constantly ask for my guidance and my support. You are coming to the realization that you know nothing, that practically everything you have been taught about me or my teaching is false and must be rejected. You know that the only way in which you can hear me is through your own heart and through the complete embrace of your experience. This is the essence of your surrender to me.

You are asking now very simply and directly for a way without fear. You are asking how to stay in the present moment. You are willing to practice what you preach. You are willing to be participants as well as observers, role models as well as teachers. There are many apostles now, far more than there were when I was physically present in your experience. Now, together, we can move to stage three and experience the big letting go — the ending of the past — and establishment of grace as the guide in our lives.

Grace and Betrayal

Am I asking you to stop all planning and thought about the future? Yes, ultimately I am. All need to think about the next moment is an attachment to the past. It is fear keeping you in fear. Recognize this. Have no illusions about your plans.

Yet also be compassionate with yourself. Your greatest responsibility is to love and be gentle with yourself at all times. Don't beat yourself up because you can't help making plans.

But watch your plans and what happens to them. And watch what happens when you can let your plans go. Plans are not, in themselves, the enemy. They are just the result of your attachment to the past.

If you must have plans, have them consciously. Watch them consciously. See if the external structure you create for your life continues to match the internal reality as it unfolds. See how you compromise yourself by taking what is true in one moment and legislating the next with it.

As you watch, you will see that some things — very few I suspect — stay the same, but most things change. The nature of mind with all its thought/feeling states is changeable. Your goal in watching is to recognize what is eternal and what is temporal in these thought/feeling states. The former must become the foundation for all structure in your life. The latter must be surrendered moment to moment.

Do not despair to discover the temporality of the mind. It is not bad and it need not be condemned. Be with the ebb and flow of your thought/feeling experience. Be present to it without judgment and it will take you beyond the very limits it seems to present. Only the attachment to mindstates creates suffering, not the mindstates themselves.

I have said to you many times: do not build upon shaky ground. Do not construct the structure of your life on the changeable. Place your faith where it alone is safe, on the bedrock of your experience. Act from a place of peace, not one of desire. For desires come and go, but peace is eternal.

Relationships that support your joy and peace and ongoing healing deserve your commitment. All others are lesson-learning devices designed to wake you up by showing you your own self-betrayal. Opportunities for abusive interactions abound. 95 percent of the psycho-emotional terrain you will encounter in this life is unsuitable for building. Some of it is harsh unforgiving rock, some of it seductive quicksand. If you value yourself, do not build your nest in these places. The betrayal you experience will not be someone else's fault, for all betrayal is self-betrayal.

Be kind to yourself. No one else can fix your life or bring to you a joy you don't already feel within your heart. Build on what you have, not on what you want. For want is an illusion that comes and goes. As soon as the desire is fulfilled, another desire replaces it. The chain of desire is endless. It always takes you away from yourself. The marsh of desire is a poor place to pour the foundation of your house.

The best relationships are easy, because each person is honored. Each person is willing to be honest. Without secrets, communication prospers. With communication, intimacy grows, and consistency is established. What is true today is also true tomorrow. And yet beyond this simple truth, tomorrow is completely unknown. This is solid ground. This is where the foundation of your life must rest.

You have heard the expression "haste makes waste." It is true. What is deeply valued has your full loving intention and attention. It is nurtured, watered, and brought into fullness and truth. It does not happen overnight. It does not happen exactly how or when you want it. It flourishes through your commitment, your constancy, your devotion. What you love prospers. If unfolds. It gets roots and wings. This is the movement of grace in your life.

You see, it is not just a question of dropping your plans, although such a move would undoubtedly bring you to the threshold of peace. It is a question of finding what is real, what is true, what is consistent and dependable in yourself. If you find this, you can offer it to another. It is in truth the only thing you can offer that is not an attack.

Find what is solid in yourself and stop looking for solidity in others. It will never come to you from the outside in. If your life is anchored in the truth of your experience, then that truth can be shared. But if you are looking for truth, or love, or salvation outside yourself, you will be disappointed again and again. Only by honoring yourself does the beloved come. Those who twist themselves into pretzels in the search for love simply push the beloved away.

Who is the beloved after all? He or she is just the mirror of your own commitment to truth. When you rest in your peace, the beloved rests within you. When you betray yourself, with anyone, the beloved mourns.

Grace rests on a tenacious commitment to yourself, a commitment that says "no" gently but firmly to all who would tempt you to trade their dream for your own. One must not only say no to the invitation to self betrayal, but say no without judgment, for the tempter cannot be blamed for one's own fall from grace.

The dream of abuse ends as soon as the victim ceases to be a victim, as soon as the dreamer wakes up and says "No. This does not feel good. Please stop!"

Your entire physical experience is an awakening to self-responsibility. You have come here to betray yourself at your brother's hands. He is simply the instrument of your self-betrayal. When you realize this, you forgive yourself and him. You release the past. You enter the present authentic and free.

I have told you that you are free to live whatever life you choose to live. "Fat chance!" you say, pointing to the chains on your feet.

"Who made those chains?" I ask.

"God did!" you angrily exclaim.

"No. It is not true. God did not make the chains. If He made them, you would never escape from the prison of your own beliefs."

Maps and Signs

When you are embarking on a journey it is helpful to look at a road map. A road map is an intellectual construction that helps you get a general sense of how to proceed. Yet it is not, and can never be, an actual description of the road. No one can tell you what the road will be like. Only your experience can do that.

There comes a point in every situation when

preparations end and the experience begins. Knowing that you have prepared well may give you confidence, but only trust in yourself enables you to excel. Trust is a big let-go into the experience. It is a leap of faith.

Eventually, everyone must put the road map down and be present in the experience. Perhaps one encounters unexpected construction, a detour, a change in weather. Driving a car is different than looking at a map.

The best that linear, sequential thinking can give you is a map of your potential experience. But it cannot guide you through that experience. When you are in the midst of the experience, there are signs that help you out. The detour sign tells you when there is a need for a change of direction. Highway signs tell you to get in the right lane or the left. There are signs telling you where there are places to eat, to sleep or to get gas. Without reading these signs you could not have a successful experience.

Signs come from the interface between outer and inner reality. They are created through our intuitive connection with life. Signs happen only in the present moment. You don't get a sign that says "go right tomorrow or sometime next month." The sign says go right now or very soon. Signs show you how to navigate in the here and now. They are extremely useful and important. Unfortunately, they are almost totally neglected by the left brain, linear mind.

When you go on a journey, a map can be very helpful. Left brain information can help you to prepare. But once you embark, signs are a necessity. Are you paying attention to the signs that arise in your life? Or are you trying to do your life with a map alone?

Each of you has access to guidance at a deep emotional level. If you will "be with" your experience, you will sense the signs that emerge. The sign may simply tell you "this feels right" or "this doesn't feel good," but that is often the only information you need. You don't need to have a vision of a saint in order to receive guidance.

Guidance is your greatest ally in life. When you rely on

your guidance, you can get by with a minimum of planning. But when you ignore your guidance, no amount of planning can guide you home.

If you know where you want to go, you can rely on your guidance to help you get there. Trying to figure out "how you will get there" intellectually is an exercise in futility. You simply can't know in advance. But when you are in process, the signs will appear, and you will know what turns to take.

The more you trust your guidance, the more spontaneous your life becomes. Plans are always tentative, allowing for unanticipated challenges and gifts. But this does not suggest that you are not fully committed. Indeed, you are able to make commitments from a deeper place. And when you fulfill these commitments you do so without sacrifice.

Re-Negotiating Commitments

Often, in the course of living, commitments need to be revised. A plan is made for the future that is not materializing. No matter how hard you try to follow the plan, it just won't come together. This is a sign to tune in, release past expectations, and be open to what wants to happen in the moment.

Re-negotiating commitments is not a sign of weakness or inconstancy unless it happens chronically. When something doesn't seem to be working for you, the best thing you can do is tell the truth to the other people involved. More often than not you will find that others have their own reservations about the plan. Revising the plan is therefore in the interest of all parties.

Sometimes you may ask for a change in commitment that won't be reciprocated by the others involved. Then, you will need to tune in and decide if this change is really important to you. Is your fulfillment of the plan really important to the other person? And can you fulfill the commitment and still honor yourself? Usually, if your

30

intention is to honor yourself and the other people, a mutually acceptable solution can be found. Holding fast to the possibility that your highest good is not in conflict with the highest good of others facilitates the discovery of solutions that honor everyone equally.

Abuse and betrayal happen when plans are held rigidly or agreements are broken in fear. If you make a commitment and don't feel comfortable keeping it, you need to communicate this to the people involved. The important thing here is not whether a promise is kept but whether a change in heart or commitment is communicated. At all times, you best honor others by telling the truth about your experience.

Betrayal happens through reactivity. Fear comes up and it is not acknowledged or communicated. The fear-driven behavior that results is an attack against others. The alternative to this is honest communication. When you say to another "I am experiencing fear and I'm not sure I can keep my commitment to you," you have honored both the other person and yourself. But if you say nothing and withdraw in fear or act in a hostile manner, you simply deepen the fear that you (and probably the other person) are experiencing.

The issue of commitment is one of the most charged issues that comes up for human beings. Fears of being controlled, abandoned or betrayed are universal. Those who demand love from others or capitulate to those demands are ultimately abandoned or betrayed. That's because they are betraying themselves.

To say "yes" or "no" to another person is a clear communication. But to say "no" and mean yes or to say "yes" and mean no creates the conditions for abuse.

To understand that you said "yes" but now know that it doesn't feel good is the first step in honoring yourself. To tell your partner is the second step.

Ultimately, no one must hold another person to a commitment made in the past which no longer feels good in the present. If you cannot release another person from the past, how can you release yourself?

What matters is not whether you come together or apart, but whether you do so in mutual honesty and respect. That is the key to it all.

Needs

Your major disconnect with the rhythm of love is the belief that there is something you can give or take from another. This belief and the manipulations that spring from it render your life painful beyond measure.

Consider why you are always disappointed in your relationships with others. Whatever you seek from another always floats up in front of you like a balloon filled with water. As soon as you prod it, demanding the love you feel you deserve, the balloon pops and you get soaked. Be honest: have you ever received from another what you wanted that person to give you? Of course not! The only reason that person came into your life was to remind you of the nurturing you need to give to yourself.

Consider why you always hit bottom whenever you try to give to, help or fix anyone else. The very need to fix someone else betrays your belief that you are not acceptable as you are.

Whenever there is "need" or compulsion in giving or receiving, you can be sure love is a long way away. When love is present, one gives and receives freely, without attachment.

That is because you can give and receive only what you have, not what you don't have. The attempt to give or get what you do not have is futile. It can end only in disappointment and sorrow.

If you are loving to someone, you will receive love, because love always returns to itself. It you demand love, you will receive demands for love. As you sow, so shall you reap.

The law of energy is circular. What goes out comes back and what comes back goes out. So how can you "get" something you do not have? It is impossible!

The truth is that you have everything that you need. Nothing that you need has been withheld from you. In this sense you can only "need" what you don't need.

Please stay with this paradox. I am not trying to confuse you.

If you "need" something, then you believe that it is not yours to give. If it is not yours to give, then how can you receive it?

If, on the other hand, you know that it is yours to give, you will give and receive it readily. And in this case you will not "need" it.

The perception of lack blocks abundance. In truth lack is not real. But the belief in lack is real. So lack is made real by the belief in it.

If you wish to demonstrate abundance, question every "need" you have. As long as you "need" something, you cannot have it. As soon as you no longer "need" it, it appears in front of you.

Nobody needs love. Nobody needs money. Nobody needs anything. But those who believe that they need, seek without finding.

This is a simple law. You cannot receive what you are unable to give, and you can't give what you are unable to receive.

Giving and receiving are the same thing. Giving is receiving. Receiving is giving. When you know this, the whole chess game falls apart. The mystery is over.

The Perception of Equality

Being in a body gives you the opportunity to explore the mistaken belief that your needs are different from the needs of others. As soon as you begin to see that your needs are the same as the needs of others, the veil begins to lift. You stop needing special treatment. You stop giving others special treatment.

What you want for one, you want for all. You do not make one person more important than others.

The perception of equality is the beginning of the transcendence of the body and the physical world. When you no longer need to hold yourself separate from others, you can serve without being attached. You can give without needing to know how the gift is being received. Service is an opportunity, not a job description. In serving, you are not the server. You cannot serve and have an identity.

You can only be helpful to the extent that you don't have an agenda. When you need to "help" others, you're just cleverly disguising your own need for help.

The goal, you see, is not to move beyond the body, or out of this dimension. The goal is to undo the belief in separation that gives rise to the perception of one body as different from others.

All bodies are essentially the same. All bodily needs are essentially the same. All emotional needs are essentially the same. All beliefs in separation are essentially the same.

When I help you, I help myself. I help my mother and father. I help my third cousin. I help the drunk on the street corner. My help goes to all who need it. Help has nothing to do with me as helper or you as helpee, other than our simple willingness to give and receive in the moment. Help is for one and for all. You cannot offer it to one without offering it to all. Nor can you offer it to all unless you offer it to one.

There is no time or distance between the one and the many. Each is contained in the other.

Two Paths of Liberation

Time and space exists only at the level of two, of comparison, judgment, separation. My body, your body. My idea, your idea. My house, your house. This is where the body begins. Without male, there would

34

be no female. Without parent, there would be no child. Without black, there would be no white. All things exist in relationship to their opposites and are indeed defined by them.

The mind that engages in comparison, engages in separation. Knowledge, in this sense, is based on separation. That is why is it impossible to "know" God. As soon as you "know" God, you lose the experience of unity.

Much of the frustration you feel on your spiritual path comes from the fact that you cannot experience something and study it at the same time. If you stand back and observe, you will not have the experience the participant does. And if you participate, you will not have the same experience as the observer.

One spiritual method asks you to become an observer. Another asks you to be a participant. Either method works, but you cannot practice both at the same time. If you want to "know," you must learn to stand back and observe. If you want to "be," you must dive into the experience.

My own teaching is oriented to those who would dive in. It is an experiential journey into the roots of abuse. You learn by making mistakes and learning from them. That is the atonement process

Blessing the Body

Whenever I point out the inherent limitations of the physical body, someone inevitably interprets my statements to mean "the body is bad, inferior, or evil." This need to reject the body is a form of attachment to it. Where there is resistance to desire, desire itself is made stronger.

The body is not bad or inferior in any way. It is simply temporal. You will never find ultimate meaning by satisfying its needs. Nor might I add will you find ultimate meaning by denying its needs. Taking care of the body is an act of grace. Preoccupation with bodily pleasures or pains is anything but graceful.

If you wish to follow the path I have laid out for you, accept your body fully and care for it diligently. When the body is loved, it does its work without complaining.

Be aware of your feelings. The feeling of guilt is often outpictured through the physical body. If you are feeling badly about something you said to a friend or family member, you might injure your mouth, tongue, or teeth, get a sore throat or laryngitis.

Be sensitive to your bodily symptoms. They show you how your body is attempting to carry out the conscious or subconscious commands it feels it has received from you.

You cannot neglect your body and learn to love yourself. Instead, embrace the body with love and it will become a willing servant to the goals of Spirit.

Even if it were possible to totally neglect the physical body, freedom would not be found. For upon the death of the physical body, another body is experienced. Each body is a sheath or a veil that holds the soul in some degree of ignorance/limitation. We are always attracted to the bodily form that allows us to fully experience our current level of fear. The more volatile our fears, the denser the body must be to contain them.

So I suggest to you the futility of trying to escape the body you are in. Accepting your body is one of the lessons of this embodiment. And this, my friends, includes your sexuality.

Let your lovemaking be a joyful act, an act of surrender to the Christ in yourself and your partner. Physical love is no less beautiful than other forms of love, nor can it be separated from them. Those who view physical love as unholy will experience it that way, not because it is, but because they perceive it that way.

If a child is born to you and your partner through the physical celebration of your love, you will not experience the entry of that child into your lives as a burden upon you. If you experience the child as a burden, then look to the quality of your relationship. The child is always the barometer for that.

36

Once the child has entered your life, he or she becomes part of the fabric of your embodiment. There is no way to escape responsibility for this relationship. It will continue throughout your lifetime. And you will use this relationship, as you use all your intimate relationships, to lessen your guilt or to intensify it. And this is true whether you remain with your partner or not.

Dogmatic rules about marriage and children are not helpful if you would walk this path. I have asked you to "love all equally." That includes your spouse and your children. If you walk away from your spouse and children without full forgiveness and completion, you are simply postponing what must inevitably happen if you are to find peace.

Does it matter how long it takes? No, not to me, but I would not be honest with you if I did not tell you that the longer you wait, the more pain you will experience.

"Is it ever right," you ask, "to take the life of an unborn child?" I must tell you that it is never right to take a life, under any circumstances. Does that mean that it will not happen? No, that is for sure. And when it does happen, one needs to have compassion for all those involved.

You do not live in a perfect world. To expect others to be perfect is to attack them. That is not my teaching. Even perceiving others as wrong is a form of attack.

Do not attack your brother or sister. Nothing good can come of it.

Religious Righteousness

Religious righteousness is attack in disguise. Only those who are full of pride think that they have exclusive understanding of the truth and the right to judge or teach others.

The Christian religion—the religion that purports to be inspired by me—is riddled with countless cases of spiritual pride. The abuse of others, under any guise, cannot be justified.

It is inevitable, I suppose, that someone will always be looking for a soapbox to stand on. And others who are uncertain in their own faith will listen to him and call him Messiah. Proclaiming his teaching, they will neglect the wisdom that lies within their own hearts. But such idols inevitably fall, and when they do the fears of the followers come to light for healing.

The one who stands on the soapbox may be foolish, but the one who listens to him is more foolish still. And more foolish than both is the one who condemns either one.

We need to learn to let others live and learn. The only help that we can offer them comes through our acceptance and love and not through our judgment.

I am not one to condemn adultery, or divorce, or abortion. For if I were to condemn these situations, those involved in them would be crucified. We would have yet another inquisition, another holy war pitting good against evil, just against unjust.

My job is not to condemn, but to understand and to bless. My job is to see the fear in people's eyes and remind them that they are loved.

If that is my job, why would I have you beat and burn and excommunicate those who are most in need of your love? You would bring me to the level of your fear, put your words in my mouth and attribute them to me. My friend, stop and behold yourself. You have misunderstood. You are mistaken. My teaching is about love, not about judgment, condemnation, or punishment.

I have given you only two rules: to love God and to love each other. Those are the only rules you need. Do not ask me for more. Do not ask me to take sides in your soap opera battles. Am I pro-life or pro-choice? How could I be one without also being the other? It is not possible.

When the truth comes to you, you will no longer need to attack your brother. Even if you think you are right and he is wrong, you will not attack him with "the truth," but offer him your understanding and your support. And together you will move closer to the truth because of the love and gentleness you share.

Every time I give a teaching, someone makes it into a stick to beat people with. Please, my friends, words that are used to beat people up cannot come from me.

I have offered you the key to door within. Please use it, and do not worry about the thoughts and actions of others. Work on yourself. When you have established the truth in your own heart, then you can go out and share that truth with others.

If you would serve this teaching, learn it first. Do not be a mouthpiece for words and beliefs you have not brought fully into the rhythms of your life. Do not appoint yourself as my foot soldier, for I have none. All who extend my teaching do so from the same level of consciousness as me. Otherwise what they extend cannot be my teaching.

A man or woman of Spirit has compassion for all beings. What she says, she demonstrates in her actions. You will not see her act unkindly toward others, or require them to follow her and do her will. True, she has an inner certainty that gives an air of authority to what she says. Yet she is forever returning that authority to her listeners. For they and they alone must choose the assumptions from which they wish to live their lives.

Part 2

Right Relationship

Heartsteps

Many of you believe that relationships will make you happy. Nothing could be further from the truth. The promise of fulfillment through relationship is a cruel hoax. That you will discover soon enough.

There is only one way that you will find genuine fulfillment in your life and that is to learn to love and accept yourself. With that as a foundation, relationships cease to be traumatic. Perhaps that is because one does not bring such intense expectations to them. When you know how to "be with" yourself, it is not so difficult to "be with" another.

But if your life is a flight from self, how can you expect any relationship to be grounded? It just is not possible. All you have are a clash of wings in a crowded sky. In your time, with the break up of both extended and nuclear family structures, more people are struggling to make contact with the ground. Existential rhythms of acceptance and love have been destroyed. Trust is barely alive in the hearts of the majority of people. This happens whenever the old dies and the new is born. It is a time of trauma and transition.

Recognize this. Do not seek outside yourself for happiness in a time of great trauma. What you catch in the net of your seeking will be more than you bargained for. Your own pain is enough to work on. Don't exacerbate it by taking on another's suffering.

If you want to dance with another, root yourself first. Learn to hear your own guidance. Dialogue with the hurt child and the divine host within. Practice forgiveness and compassion for yourself. Be with your experience and learn from it. Stay in the rhythm of your life. Be open to others, but do not go out of your way to find them. Those who know how to dance will meet you half way. It will not be a struggle. You will feel companionship without effort.

This is how it should be. If you are at peace with your

partner, you are in right relationship. If you are not at peace, then your relationship is inappropriate or premature.

Inappropriate relationships exacerbate the abuse patterns of the past. Learning in such meetings is painful. A better choice can and should be made. But in order to make that better choice, one must be able to ask unabashedly for what one wants. If you let another dictate the terms of the relationship, don't be surprised if you don't feel honored.

You know what feels good to you and what does not. Say what you need, speak your truth, and be firm in your commitment to your own healing. Only through your commitment to honor yourself can you attract a partner willing to do the same.

These are simple truths. But they are not practiced. Over and over again, you compromise, play by other people's rules, and betray yourself. By now, you should be tired of repeating the lesson and exacerbating the wound.

I will say this to you as clearly as I can: If you do not know how to take care of yourself, and if you are not willing to do so, nobody else will take care of you. Your lack of love and commitment to yourself attracts people with similar lessons into your vibrational field. Then you will simply mirror back to each other that lack of self-understanding and self-commitment.

Commitment to another is impossible without commitment first to self. This is important. Those who try to act in a selfless way are putting the cart before the horse. Embrace the self first and then you can go beyond it. What I am suggesting is not selfishness. It is the ultimate surrender to the divine within.

The beloved comes into being with the commitment to self. He or she manifests outwardly as soon as that commitment is trustworthy. Then the outer commitment and the inner one go together. In worshipping the beloved, one worships the divine self that lives in many bodies. This is sacred relationship

Few meet the beloved in this life, for few have learned

to honor themselves and heal from the inside out. However, you can be one of these few if you are willing to commit to your own healing. Make that commitment and the beloved is put on notice.

Take this simple vow: I pledge that I will no longer betray or violate myself in any relationship. I will communicate how I think and feel honestly, with compassion for the other, but without attachment to how he or she receives my communication. I trust that by telling the truth and honoring myself, I am in communion with the beloved. I will no longer try to "make a relationship work" by sacrificing myself to try to meet my partner's needs.

Marriage

Marriage must begin first in the hearts of both partners. All committed relationships have one thing in common — one wishes the best for the other person. One is willing even to give the partner up if she or he could thereby find a greater happiness. Contrary to popular belief, marriage is not a tie that binds but one that releases.

One wants the greatest happiness for the partner in the same way that one wants the greatest happiness for oneself. One loves the partner as one loves oneself, with an equal love.

In a true partnership, the partner's needs are as important as one's own. Not more important. Not less important. But equally important.

Marriage extends to the partner the same caring, loving intention with which one embraces oneself. It is not a new gesture, but an extension of a familiar one.

Marriage is not a promise to be together throughout all eternity, for no one can promise that. It is a promise to be present "now." It is a vow that must be renewed in each moment if it is to have meaning.

In truth, you can be married in one moment and not in

the next. Marriage is therefore a process, a journey of becoming fully present to oneself and the other.

All couples would do well to remember frequently what their commitment is. To lose sight of the commitment is to desecrate the marriage. Adulterous affairs are just the unfortunate outcome of a lack of intimacy between the partners. They are not the problem, but the symptom of the problem.

When you are truly committed to your partner, it is impossible to betray him or her. For to betray the partner is like betraying the self. You just cannot do it.

You may experience an attraction to another person, but you do not have a desire to be with that other person. You do not fantasize about what it would be like to take that person to bed.

When you are married, the urge to sexual union is an important part of the sacrament. Marriage is meant to be a full-chakra embrace. Sexual passion is part of a greater attraction to be with the person. Whenever it splits off, sex becomes an attack.

Many married people engage in non-devotional sex. This is the beginning of a process of fragmentation that often culminates in infidelity. However, this could not happen unless one first desecrated the relationship with the partner by engaging in non-loving, non-surrendered sex.

When love is mutual and the partners are surrendered to one another emotionally, sexuality is completely uplifting and sacred. Nothing outside could threaten the relationship.

But when communication in the relationship becomes careless and shoddy, when time is not taken for one-to-one intimacy, the relationship becomes a shell in which one hides. Energy and commitment disappear from the relationship. And sex becomes an act of physical betrayal.

Communion can be restored if there is mutual willingness and trust. For the goal of full-chakra union is realized entirely through love, energy and attention.

Divorce

Relationships ultimately end themselves. The energy and interest is simply not there anymore. The road to divorce begins with the recognition that there is no longer a shared purpose and a mutual energetic attraction.

Not all relationships are meant to be marriages. Some are temporary learning experiences lasting a few months or a few years. Unfortunately, people marry before they know in their hearts they have found a lifetime partner. But, as long as the mistake is mutually acknowledged, no harm is done.

Shame about making a mistake in marriage does not serve anyone. Lots of people make these mistakes. Some people suffer with their mistakes, staying in relationships long after they have lost their sacredness. Others bail out of their relationships too soon, before they have learned their lessons and come to completion with their partners.

This is not a new story.

Divorce, like marriage, begins first in the hearts of the partners. It is an organic process of dis-entanglement. When people have gone as far together as they are capable of or willing to go, divorce is the only humane solution. It is unethical to try to hold another person against his or her will. At best, the divorce happens in the context of gratitude toward the partner for the time shared. As such, it is not a separation, but a completion.

It would be dishonest to suggest that children are not wounded by the divorce of their parents. On the other hand, they are also wounded by the unwillingness of their parents to love and respect each other. If the detachment of divorce helps the partners to come back into mutual respect, then it can be progressive for the children. Children benefit whenever they see adults acting in a loving and respectful manner to one another. However, in a healing divorce situation, parents must focus intently on providing consistent attention to the children so that they do not feel abandoned or to blame. The importance of this cannot be overemphasized.

Process and Boundaries

Learning to be in a relationship requires an understanding of boundaries. You need to understand what psychological material belongs to you so that you don't project your fears and insecurities onto your partner or, if you do, you know how to take them back. Nothing is more confusing in a relationship than the cycle of mutual, reactive projections. While the mirroring process — seeing your own qualities in the other person — may be helpful, most people do not have a developed enough sense of boundaries to use this kind of feedback skillfully. For most people, projection results not in greater consciousness, but in more unconscious reactiveness. While the pain of this may eventually lead to greater consciousness, there are gentler ways to learn.

To learn gently, choose a partner who does not push all of your buttons at once. Choose a partner who desires a conscious relationship and is willing to take responsibility for facing his or her fears. Choose a partner you like and respect, a partner who can hold a safe, loving space for you. Do not settle for less.

Then begin to practice the following simple process whenever you and your partner are not experiencing peace in your relationship.

1. Identify your fear. Fear is at the root of all negative, stressful emotions, including anger and hurt. Be with your feelings long enough to identify the root fear. Exaggerate the fear if necessary.

2. Identify how you see yourself as a victim. Peace leaves our hearts only when we think it is possible for someone else to do something to us against our will. How specifically do you feel powerless in this situation?

3. *Own the fear and the feelings of victimhood* and state them to the other person in a way that takes total responsibility for your experience. *(eg. When you didn't call, I felt afraid that I was going to be abandoned. I feel weak and powerless when I depend on you to love me in a particular way.)* Ask the person to listen to what you say without judging it or responding to it.

4. *Check to see if the person understood you,* so that you can feel completely heard.

5. *Ask the person if he or she has any feelings (not judgments or defenses) about what you have communicated.*

6. *Listen without judgment or interpretation* to what the person shares with you and acknowledge that you heard it.

7. *Thank each other for making the space to listen.*

8. *Don't try to resolve anything now. Just feel good about hearing each other. Agree to talk again if either of you has more feelings or some insight into what happened.*

This process always works because it helps both of you take total responsibility for your feelings in any situation. It doesn't allow you to make the other person responsible for what you are feeling or vice versa. When you "own" what you are feeling and communicate it, the other person does not feel attacked, because you are disclosing information about yourself rather than blaming him or her for your experience. This keeps appropriate boundaries intact and does not invite mutual trespass.

The process also succeeds because it does not focus on "fixing" either the other person or yourself. The only outcome that is desired here is increased communication (in a non-threatening way) of what each person is feeling. Honest, heart-to-heart communication immediately restores the feeling of love and connection. When that happens, all problems — which are merely symptoms of separation and disconnection — disappear.

Trying to focus on the problem merely reinforces it. The energy goes to "fixing" the separation rather than understanding its cause. All need to fix comes from an assumption that something is wrong. And if something is wrong, usually "someone" is made wrong. It is more healing to start with the assumption that nothing is wrong. You just have a feeling you are holding which you need to communicate.

Holding back feelings is the beginning of separation. Sharing them is the ending of it. This is the ebb and flow of all relationships. But most holding immediately goes into projection and blame. And so peace quickly moves beyond one's immediate reach.

In those moments, one needs to take the projection back, "own" the feeling and take responsibility for communicating it. That simple act brings back appropriate boundaries and creates a safe space in which others can hear us and we too can be heard.

Daily Rituals of Intimacy and Peace

Just as the quality of your relationship with yourself can be measured by the amount of time you consciously give to "being" with yourself, so the quality of your relationship with another can be measured by the amount of time you consciously give to "being" together. For example, if you find it helpful to spend a half an hour in silence or meditation on a daily basis, you might want to consider doing the same with your partner. Or if you enjoy eating out or making a nice leisurely dinner at home, why not do the same thing with your partner?

Find ways to honor and take care of yourself while being with your partner. Communicate to your partner what is peaceful and nurturing for you. Choose certain rituals which sustain you both to practice together on a daily and weekly basis.

Each day celebrate your commitment to each other by spending at least five minutes of quiet time looking silently into each other's eyes. Practice softening the hard shell of your life and letting your partner's love in. Remember why you chose to walk with this being at your side and reconfirm your commitment to his or her highest good. Start the day with the gift of your love for each other. And then offer it to God. Pray for a day of learning, loving, and self-disclosure. Pray to open your heart to each person who comes into your life. Pray to walk through your fears. Pray to be of help. Pray to listen for your guidance.

Each day remember each other and remember God. In this way, the spiritual purpose of your partnership is renewed.

Each night before you go to bed repeat this ritual. Give thanks for all that happened that day to help you open your heart and walk through your fears. Give any unresolved issues back to God with your willingness to do what is for the highest good of all concerned. Let any uneasiness with your partner be cleared verbally or non-verbally. Express your gratitude for each other. Looking into each other's eyes, let your heart be open. Move into making love with your partner by opening your eyes and your heart to his or her beauty. Move into making love with gratitude and celebration.

Sex is not something to be rushed or "gotten over with." You do not have to go unconscious to enjoy the stimulation of foreplay or the release of orgasm with your partner. Sex with your partner is sacred. It is an act of trust, of mutual pleasure, of bodily communion.

Sex as Bodily Communion

The enjoyment of your sensuality is essential for the full unfolding of your relationship. It is nothing to be afraid of or ashamed of. It is to be celebrated as a gift from God. Having a partner who loves you, cherishes you, touches you with gratitude and abandon is nothing other than a divine gift.

Some people oppose healthy sexuality because they have trouble accepting their own sexuality. These people — including many clergy — would poison the waters for others. Pay them no mind. They have their own difficult lessons in this life.

The only sexual expression that is reprehensible is sex without love. Some people are addicted to this kind of object-oriented sex. They try to find their satisfaction through the pleasure of orgasm. This never works, because after the peak of every orgasm is the trough of existential contact with the partner. If you love the person you are with, the trough will be a peaceful, comforting space. If you do not love the person, the trough will feel hollow and uncomfortable.

Sex without love is ultimately unsatisfactory and addictive. More will always be needed. More sex, more partners, more stimulation. But more is never enough. When you engage in sexual activity with someone you do not love, you dishonor yourself and the other person.

Sex without love lays the foundation for abuse. If you wish to save yourself much grief, do not engage in sexual behavior with someone you don't love. Even if you are in a loving partnership, do not engage in sexual behavior when your heart is not open to your partner. Sex without love, under any guise, fragments the energy of your union and exacerbates your emotional wounds.

This is common sense, yet how many of you practice it? Don't be sloppy in your behavior with your partner. Don't close your eyes and go unconscious. The beloved deserves your full attention.

Weekly Rituals

Once per week, gather together with others in fellowship to remember the divine within each of you. In our tradition, the Sabbath has always been a holy time. It is a time when the whole community assembles to remember its vow to take its direction from God.

On the Sabbath, you take a break from the ebb and flow of worldly affairs. You give thanks to God for all the joys in your life and you ask His help in meeting the challenges. Together you pray for understanding and peace. Together you create a safe space where people may open their hearts and move through their fears.

Honesty and self-disclosure are welcomed in a non-judgmental, mutually supportive atmosphere. Suffering is acknowledged, shared, and released. No block or dis-ease standing between you and another is allowed to remain heavy on your heart or his. This is a place of confession and atonement. It is a place where the misfortunes and misunderstandings of your worldly experience can be righted in the forgiving light of unconditional acceptance and love.

Here the couple and the nuclear family find the extended family — the community — the microcosmic global village containing a diversity of human beings: black and white, old and young, male and female, rich and poor, educated and untaught. Here the individual's heart is open to all her brothers and sisters. Here he declares his equality and his solidarity with other women and men.

In every community, there should be such a safe, loving, non-judging space open to all. If there is no such space in your city or town, perhaps this is where your ministry begins.

In reaching out to meet your need for spiritual community, you create a pathway for others to find the safe, healing space. The simple pre-requisite is your willingness to join with another human being in the goal of loving and supporting each other unconditionally.

This is not a political act, but an act of the spirit. It must necessarily be open to all who would agree to practice its simple guidelines. There is no soapbox here, no podium for self-important teachers to preach their personal gospels.

This is not a place where beliefs are espoused, but where the principles of love and equality are practiced. It is a place of forgiveness, a place where we are safe to leave the past behind and open up to the miracle of the present moment. It is a simple place, a safe place, a place that is easily found and easily maintained.

Leave all of your others idols and gods behind when you enter the door of this sanctuary. Leave behind all your struggles for self-worth, approval, money, or fame. Here recognition is given to you freely and without conditions. Here you are an equal child of God, a brother or a sister to each one who gathers with you.

Support the community with your loving commitment: your time, your energy, the money you earn using your skills and talents. When every member gives according to his or her ability, sufficient resources are gathered to support the place and its programs of service to the congregation and the community.

Remember, keep it small and keep it simple. To maintain intimacy and integrity, spiritual communities should not exceed one hundred active adult members. Anything larger than this becomes an institution and ceases to be responsive to the needs of its members.

A children's program should provide hands-on instruction to children in how to take responsibility for their thoughts and feelings, how to communicate honestly without attacking others, and how to resolve conflicts peacefully. Principles of meditation, prayer, and healing can be explained and demonstrated. But the primary focus of the program should be on how to honor oneself and others equally. Non-competitive games, drama, art and music can provide the vehicle for self expression and cooperation.

The simplest form of spiritual community is the affinity group,* a group of eight to ten people who are committed to practicing forgiveness and learning to love and support each

*For more information about affinity groups write to the Miracles Community Network, P.O. Box 181, S. Deerfield, MA 01373

other unconditionally. The affinity group is a new-paradigm spiritual community. It has a facilitator rather than a leader or teacher. And eventually, the facilitation role is shared by all involved.

A more diverse spiritual community can be formed by bringing affinity groups together. The individuals in these groups already know how to create a safe, loving space together, so their experience supports the expression of this process in a wider context. Once a month, four times per year, or whenever the Spirit moves, the groups can join together for a pot-luck dinner and group meditation. In this way, the larger spiritual community evolves organically.

Holding Each Other's Innocence

The purpose of an affinity group or of any spiritual community is to hold a vision of everyone's innocence. In an authentic spiritual community, the safe, loving, space is inclusive, open to all who are willing to join together in holding the space. Those unwilling to hold the space should be released with love, prayed for and told that they are welcome back when they can be committed to the purpose and guidelines of the group. Protecting the safety of the space is as important as holding the door open to new members. Unless the space is held vigilantly, the unconditionally loving and supportive dynamics of the group will be needlessly threatened.

Members of the spiritual community desire to be loved and accepted by others without conditions and are willing to do the same for others. The unconditional innocence of each member is held, regardless of what that person shares. Past mistakes, transgressions, misunderstandings, no matter how seemingly severe are not held against the person. In every moment, that person is seen as new, innocent, unstained. Every tendency one has to judge or condemn is seen for what it is: as guilt projected on another. As soon as the projection is recognized, it is owned. "I see you as selfish because I have acted in a selfish way in the past and I have not yet forgiven myself for it. "

When self-forgiveness happens, there is no longer anything to condemn another person for. The spiritual community therefore simply holds the safe space for self-forgiveness to happen. In that sense, it is not an interactive process. Nobody is trying to change, fix, or heal anyone else. Healing is done by the Spirit in the instant the individual is willing to stop playing the role of victim and asks for help.

The group holds the space in which addictions and control can be yielded up to Spirit. It does not pretend to have the answer for any of its members. It simply extends to each individual again and again the recognition of his innocence. The group sees the individual as I would see her. She is acceptable as she is right now. No matter what else she seems to be asking for, all she wants is love and I am willing to love her. In my Christhood, I call all the members of the group to theirs.

See that all that is requested is love and acceptance and give it freely and abundantly. Receive the same when it is offered to you. When you do this, you will experience such grace and overwhelming bliss, you will have a hard time staying in your body. Your mind will be surrendered and free of judgments and you will feel connected to others with a profound intimacy that cannot be put into words. As you surrender to God's ever present love by extending it to yourself and others, you will cease to perceive separate forms. Each person you meet will be the Beloved, the opportunity to give and receive without conditions. Each fear that arises in your mind, contracting your heart, will be a moment of darkness given gladly to the light.

You will learn to hold your innocence with absolute conviction and, as you do, you will hold it not just for yourself, but for all of God's children. For you are the light of the world. There is no other. There is no awakening separate from your experience. There is nothing beyond you for which you must seek. There is nothing in the past for which you must atone. There is just this moment in which you shine brightly like a star illuminating the dark sky. Wherever you look, new stars are exploding into light. The inner experience and the outer experience have joined into one pulsating rhythm. It is the song of all things, the poem of thought breaking open at dawn. It is the phoenix rising from your now painless death. It is your risen soul, your Christself, your innocence.

Undoing Shame

As long as there are judgments being made, there will be shame in the world. Shame is the belief that what is false is true. It is the upside down perception of the world. Shame says "I am bad." This is not true and it can never be true. Yet you believe it, and you project that belief on all your brothers and sisters. Every time you make a judgment of another human being, you are re-reinforcing your own shame.

Peace will not come to the world until it comes into your own heart. And it cannot come into your heart as long as you see enemies or "evil" people outside of you. Every evil you perceive in the world points to an unforgiving place in your own heart that is calling out for healing. Stop judging others. Stop the game of blame. See every judgment for what it is: an attack against yourself, an attack against God's son, a deepening of your own shame.

You, my friend, are the only son of God, just as I was. Apart from your beliefs and your experience, there is no world. Apart from your judgments there is no hell. Apart from your love, there is no heaven.

Yet you pretend to be a victim of that world. You pretend there is a "devil" apart from your beliefs, or an "evil" not connected to your judgments. It is not true. Every evil comes from your judgments and every devil comes from the projection of your shame.

Do not see the drama happening outside of you or you

will lose the key to the kingdom. Those who see themselves as victims will not be empowered. Those who see themselves as weak will not overcome the obstacles in their lives.

The drama of shame and blame is happening only in your mind and that is where it must be shifted. Believe for a moment "I am lovable; I am acceptable; I am worthy;" and your victimhood comes to an end. Believe "I am capable of loving my brother regardless of how he acts toward me" and the invisible bonds of projection will fall away. You are the one who holds the key to the kingdom. I invite you to use it. Give the love you have to give and the love you yearn for will return to you, perhaps when you least expect it. The gift of forgiveness you give to yourself extends to all human beings. Gradually, the chain of shame and blame is transformed into bridges of forgiveness.

Between every body that seems to separate one mind from another, a bridge is born. Between the thought "I am not worthy of love" and "he is unloving to me" a bridge of self-worth is constructed that only the righteous can cross.

What you are willing to give to others you give to yourself. If you offer committed love, love that overlooks faults and soars above judgments, how can any less be returned to you?

This is a circular world. What goes out comes back in and vice versa. It only appears to be linear. It only appears to exist in time and space. But in truth thought and action are simultaneous. There is no "out there." Here and there dwell together. As soon as you have the thought "I am not worthy" an experience will come in to confirm that thought. This is not a punishment from God, but a testimony to the power of your mind.

Do not blame God for the apparent misfortune you receive. Do not blame your neighbor, or your spouse or your child. Do not even blame yourself. Simply ask to see it free of judgment, as it truly is. See how you called for it and it faithfully answered your call. See this without beating yourself. See this without beating the stranger who came to your door to deliver the message. Just see it in surrender, in reconciliation with your self and your experience.

God comes to you in many forms. Everything that happens in your life is part of your God experience. If your experience feels painful, ask "what can I learn from this pain?" Do not ask the pain to go away. Do not reject the lesson. For every lesson turned away comes again in another guise. Ask instead "What would you have me learn, dear Lord?"

The Father and Mother of Creation ask only for what contributes to your awakening. For they have awakened and they wish the same for you. Their love for you is both gentle and fierce. One type of love is not enough. The love of both father and mother are necessary.

Pray to Father for courage and to Mother for gentleness. With courage, walk through your fears. With gentleness, open your heart.

You are blessed to have two parents who love you. If you do not know this, you simply have more to forgive.

Forgiving the Parents

Your relationship with Father/Mother God depends to a large extent upon willingness to your heal with your parents and get on with your life. If you are still blaming your parents for the difficulties of your life, your connection to God will remain difficult and unstable. Your anger and sense of betrayal in reference to your parents cannot help but be carried forward to your experience of God. If you believe that you are a victim, then you also believe that God is your abuser. Who but an abuser would not rescue his child from danger?

Is your problem with the male or female principle, with the father or the mother, or both? Problems with the male principle translate into an inability to understand and fulfill one's creative life purpose. Problems with the female principle translate into an inability to develop loving, intimate, relationships. Generally, when there is a problem on one side of the equation, there is an overcompensation on the other. Balance can only be restored by honoring both parents and their contribution to your awakening, no matter how difficult that contribution seemed.

And lest this remain unclear, I would have you realize that there is no human being who has not been abused by a parent. All unconscious behavior is abusive. All behavior which is compulsive stems from unhealed, unconscious places within the person's mind and experience. And every parent on earth has such places of unconsciousness. It is all a matter of degree. No parent can honor you totally unless he has learned totally to honor himself. And no one who takes physical embodiment has reached that stage of self-forgiveness.

I have asked you "who will cast the first stone?" When you are about to point the finger of accusation against one of your brothers or sisters who has acted in an abusive way toward you or another who is dear to you, ask "how can I judge? How can I know the painful and unloved place from which this act has arisen? How can I know except through the depths of my own pain and separation?" And if you will dwell there, instead of from some false place of moral superiority, you will feel compassion for the ones in pain, for both the abused and the abuser.

Whatever abuse you have experienced in your life must ultimately be forgiven. When it is forgiven, you no longer hold onto the violation. You release the shame. First you forgive yourself. Then you forgive your abuser. Do not try to do it the other way around. You cannot extend forgiveness to another until you have claimed it for yourself.

When you are complete with your parents, you will stop creating parental lessons in your intimate relationships. You will end the cycle of unconscious, reactive abuse and move your healing into a conscious arena with a partner who is able to do the same.

Your parents' relationship presented you with a psycho-emotional learning gestalt. You moved into physical embodiment with your parents and siblings because they provided the best available classroom in which you could learn to honor yourself and others equally. All the ways in which you had to bargain for love were lessons in integrity and self-responsibility. All the ways in which you felt controlled, abused, or abandoned, and all the ways you defended yourself by attacking or withholding your love were likewise lessons in self-empowerment and equality.

When you come to peace with your parents and accept them as equals, then your healing of the past is complete. This means that you no longer wish them to change to meet your expectations, nor do you feel any desire to change to meet their expectations. You rest in mutual acceptance and affection. You no longer accept any claims of authority from them nor do you make any claim of authority over them. As equals, you bless them. You respect their achievements and have compassion for their challenges and mistakes.

The soul-mate or life partner comes in when your parental lessons are resolved. Then the man stops finding his mother in his wife and trying to be her husband, and the woman stops finding her father in her husband and trying to be his wife. Unconscious, abusive relationships come to an end or transform themselves and the stage is set for the journey of conscious, committed intimacy.

Meeting the Soul-Mate

A soul-mate relationship is an exploration of the dynamics of equality, mutual trust and respect. It is a mature, consciously loving relationship. It requires good communication skills, generally learned through the forgiveness process in previous, less conscious relationships. In a sense, all of one's previous relationships prepare one for full participation in this relationship.

The soul-mate cannot manifest until there is honesty and clarity in all of your relationships. If you are abandoning a previous marriage partner or your children in order to be with a new lover, you might as well face facts.

You cannot find the soul-mate by abandoning any other human being. You must be right with all of your relationships. You must speak the truth fearlessly, but with great gentleness and compassion. Others need to know where you stand. They need to know how your commitment to them has changed and how it has remained the same. You demonstrate your love for them by having no secrets, by full disclosure of your thoughts and feelings. You treat them as you would wish to be treated if the situation were reversed. And so you are able to move on without abandoning, without acting in a careless, impulsive manner.

Genuine love for one person never results in unkind behavior toward another. This does not mean that you cannot revise your commitments. But it does mean that you enter the process of revision with respect and concern for the other, as well as with clarity about what you want.

When the lifepartner manifests in your life, commitment will happen as a matter of course. Your mutual desire to be in one another's presence becomes the continual, spontaneous demonstration of your commitment to each other. Where decision making with previous partners was arduous and characterized by continued ego struggle, decision making with the soul-mate is without effort. Each partner completely honors the other's thoughts and feelings without dishonoring his or her own experience. There is a willingness to be fully present, to listen for guidance together, and to make decisions only when both people feel clarity has come.

Until you have learned to listen to your guidance, you will not meet your soul-mate. Indeed, the discovery of your soul-mate happens because you are internally directed toward him or her. When you meet, you recognize the fact internally. You "know" in every cell of your being.

In the mutual acknowledgement of the life partner comes a shift in the ground of being. No longer do you live just for your own peace and happiness. But your peace and happiness expands to include the peace and happiness of the partner. Individual guidance becomes less important than mutual guidance. The focus ceases to be on how you are different, but on what you share. You enter a new stage in your life journey. One becomes externalized as two, and two become inner directed as one.

"You" are now a different entity. True, you still have a separate body, but even bodily separation begins to fade as the two of you dovetail and entwine in the act of physical and emotional love. Your minds surrender their separate longings and join in the dance of common purpose and wordless understanding. A new being is being born through you. It is the fruit of your love, and the servant of your mutual guidance.

Out of your union comes a work that could not be accomplished till now. Your joining makes it possible. Together, you accept your spiritual purpose, and fulfill it gracefully as your relationship unfolds and radiates love to all the people in your experience.

Once you meet the beloved in form, your life cannot continue on as it was. All that is separately held must be released. Only what is held together in mutual honoring and embrace can be carried forward. The isolated self must die. The self as partner, as life mate is born. This is spiritual marriage.

As more of you enter the path of self-healing and self-discovery, there is more potential for sacred union. You and others like you come together as equal partners and begin to model what the new paradigm relationship is. You and your partner radiate mutual trust and respect. You radiate shared purpose and commitment without sacrifice. You demonstrate what it means to hold a safe, loving, non-judgmental space for one another.

Spiritual Communities

Gradually, those who join in sacred union will be guided into small affinity communities of people committed to holding a safe, loving space for each other. In the course of supporting each other unconditionally, a group consciousness will spontaneously emerge and the group will be guided in a consensual fashion toward the fulfillment of the spiritual purpose made possible by the joining together of its members. Committed love always extends without effort to others who are becoming ready to receive it. Each community is therefore not only gifted with its own integral, ritual communion, but with service to others outside the group.

The extension of the safe, loving space happens naturally. There is never any urgency about it. It is not a "doing," but an allowing. Since there is no doing, there is no attachment to the outcome. That is why it is genuine service.

If there is ever any need to reach out, proselytize, convert, or build membership in the spiritual community, the space will no longer be safe either for those who pretend to hold it, or for the people toward whom it has been offered.

Growth happens because there is a natural tendency for that which is loving and healing to attract that which needs healing and love. Since this happens magnetically, there is no need to go seeking outside. But when new members are attracted to the community, there is a commitment to welcome, to acknowledge, to serve. Often this can be done best by showing others how to create and hold a safe, loving space for themselves. The environments in which this is needed are endless: schools, hospitals, shelters, prisons, you name them. When the requests come in, they are simply honored, for there is a willingness to share one's joy with all who ask for it.

As love is naturally and organically extended, and guidance increasingly functions through group consensus, the safe, loving space becomes established in the world. Separation is quietly but profoundly overcome as people find safety and reach for the love they want. A spiritual renaissance begins on the planet, born of the decision to love and honor oneself, extending into sacred relationships with another person, and finally manifesting in small, decentralized communities guided through group consensus and the mutual practice of the forgiveness process.

This scenario is given to you not because there is any need to "make" it happen, but so you will recognize what is possible for you as consciousness shifts on the planet. The age of the individual is coming to an end. As the needs of the individual are met through the commitment to self care, the capacity for genuine intimacy unfolds. Sacred relationships are formed and abusive relationships are transformed. Communities are born when several families come together. They may or may not live together, but they do join in common purpose.

The Lord has many projects for those who wish to serve. But before those projects can be assigned, the relationship commitments must be present. Those commitments literally hold the energy that is required to serve the needs of others who are reaching out for love.

You and I are all channels through which God's love can flow to others. There is no mystery in this. As soon as you make space for God in your heart, He brings the stranger to your doorstep. As soon as you make space for God in your relationship, he brings the abused and the abuser for counseling. As soon as you make space for God in your affinity community, he brings the outcasts and the disenfranchised into the sanctuary of your church.

That is the way of Spirit. When you offer love, those who are in need of that love will find you. Your job is simply to maintain the integrity of what you offer. Keep the space safe for yourself and others. Practice forgiveness and be compassionate with each other. Do not interpret another's experience or pretend to know for him or her. But honor whatever is offered with love and respect. Make a space for each brother and sister in your heart. That is how he or she is brought to God. Through your loving presence.

There was a time when I offered to be the door for you. That time is over. Now you too must become the door.

Part 3

No
Other Gods

The Door to the Divine Presence

The door to the Divine Presence opens through your heart. It opens through your kindness to yourself. It opens through your gentle acceptance of yourself in any moment. It opens through your embrace of your experience, through your willingness to be with whatever is happening in this moment.

The door to the Divine Presence opens through your kindness and gentle acceptance of others as they are in this moment. It opens through your willingness to be with them whatever they are thinking and feeling without judging them or trying to fix them. It opens through the attention and the blessings you freely and heartfully extend toward others.

The door to the Divine Presence opens through your simple remembrance of God in any moment. It opens when you know that you are not alone, that every decision you make can be given over to God. The door opens when you no longer need to be in charge of your life, when you no longer need to make reality fit your pictures of how it should be. It opens when you can surrender everything you think you know and come to each moment empty of expectations.

The door to the Divine Presence opens when you are fully alive. And in that moment, you are aligned with God. You are the one through whom God speaks and listens. You are the one.

If you want to find God, greet her now. Stop looking for her in sacred books and religious practices. That is not where you will find Her. If you want to find God, open your heart. Be gentle with yourself and others. See your judgments for what they are: the obstacle to peace within and peace without.

God is not some abstraction, but a living presence in your life that you can experience. Yet, She is not like any other living presence, because She is not in form. If you want to understand what God is, think of someone close to you who has died. That person is no longer in form, yet the essence of that person remains with you. God is the essence of all beings. She is the very breath with which all form is animated. She is the ultimate inclusive understanding, the ultimate blessing of love on all things. If you felt close to your friend, can you imagine how close you will feel to God if you will just let Her in?

How do you let Her in? It is very simple, really. Stop resisting your experience. Stop withholding your love and pushing the love of others away. Stop playing the victim. Stop blaming others for your grief or your pain. Open to it all. Let it all in. Own it. Be with it. Tell the truth about your pain. Let yourself feel the pain of others without trying to fix them. Be with it all. And She will be with you, because you trusted Her. You trusted in the intuitive perfection of your life and the lives of others. You stopped blaming and complaining. You stopped finding fault. You stopped being a hurt, angry kid. You stopped trying to punish the world for abandoning you. You stopped throwing your tantrum and just looked into Her eyes. And She winked and said: "Welcome home."

You are already home in God's love. You are already here. Take some time to be present. Breathe and be here now. Elaborate rituals of prayer and meditation are not necessary. Just breathe and be.

Be in the silence of your own heart. Let your thoughts come and go until the space between them opens. Let your feelings of anxiety, boredom, frustration come and go until a softness comes into your heart, a patience with yourself, a forgiveness that rides in and out on each breath. Let peace come into your heart, all by itself. As you allow space to be there without needing to fill it, feel the presence that comes in. That is the Spirit of God, Grace, call it what you will. It abides in you and with you now, for you have left striving behind. You have left your judgments and wounds like empty shoes at the threshold of this sacred space. In your heart now, there is only love, only blessings. And so you rest in God and She in you. This is the divine embrace.

Once you have tasted the absolute joy of this communion, you will not want to be without it. You will find a few moments every day to breathe and be, to let the world spill out from your mind, to let peace come into your heart. You will do this not out of duty or the search for approval but because it is sheer bliss. You will make time for God in the same way that you make time to embrace your lover at night. Because it feels so good. Because it is such a deep blessing.

Because God is a living presence in your life, not an abstraction. Because She offers you an ongoing relationship, a companionship that goes beyond the limits of form. Because when everything else dissolves, Her presence remains with you. Because you and She are of one mind and share the same bottomless heart.

The Only Authority

Do not expect your relationship with God to look like anyone else's or you will sabotage the relationship. God's presence in your life is totally unique. Your conversation with Her may be verbal or nonverbal, a canvas of colorful shapes or imageless. Don't try to measure your spirituality by comparing what happens for you with what happens for others.

Don't accept any intermediary between you and God. Reject all gurus and teachers. Don't accept any concepts of God that come from others. Reject magical thinking. Let go of potions and formulas. Forget what you think you know. Forget what you have been taught. Come to God empty and surrendered. Leave your petitions and agendas behind. Be with Her without expectations. Just be and let Her find you as you are, in your simple essence.

This is a time when all the idols must be rejected. All

forms of external authority must be stripped of their power. Do not make the mistake of thinking that someone else has more spiritual knowledge than you do. That is preposterous. Anyone who is close to God knows that it is you who gives God permission to be present in your life, only you. The attachment to the ideas and concepts of others interferes with the clarity of your direct connection to Spirit.

Cultivate your relationship with God directly. Enter the silence of your own heart. Talk to God. Pray and ask for guidance. Open the dialogue and listen for God's answers within and in the signs that She sends into your life.

Get to know God in your own experience. Accept no substitutes. Forget the priests, the psychics, the shamans who would give you answers. They are the blind leading the blind.

And know absolutely that any message of fear does not come from God or from any of Her ministers. Any message that disempowers you or puts you down comes from a false prophet, a manipulator, an avenger. Turn away from such teachings, but send love and compassion to those who uphold them, for they are in great pain. Show them gently through your own example that there is another way, a way of the heart, a way of simple direct experience.

Neither take teachers nor be one. Be a brother or a sister instead. Prescribe not for others nor let them prescribe for you. Prescribe not even for yourself, but listen to the voice of God and be guided by it. For you do not know. Your brother and sister do not know. Only God knows.

Only God knows. Accept no substitutes. Raise no idols before Her. Forget your astrologies, your Kabbalahs, your psychologies and your physics. None of these systems can give you the answers you seek. None of them can lead you to peace.

Burn your bibles, your channeled documents and your holy books. They are someone else's experience. Accept no other teacher or teaching than the one of your heart. That alone is God's teaching.

Do not take communion in a hall where fools preside

and the flock are mentally and spiritually asleep. Those who wish to be told what to do will find out soon enough that no one has the answers for them. Do not be one of those who gives your power up to impostors. Accept only God's teaching into your life and take communion in the silence where you meet Her.

You, my friend, are enough. You are sufficient. All the jewels of knowledge can be found within your own mind. All the joys of spirit can be discovered in your own heart.

Gather with others in mutual appreciation and gratitude to God, but do not take direction from one another. Instead, honor each other's experience. It is sacred. It is holy. It is beyond comment or evaluation.

Celebrate your common experience. Meditate and pray together. Break bread together. Give, receive, serve together. But accept no other authority in your life but God's.

Each of you is guided in a unique way and has unique gifts to offer. Celebrate that guidance and those gifts. But do not try to give your guidance to another and do not accept another's guidance if he offers it to you. That is a false gift. For what works for one will not necessarily work for another.

When you understand that you have direct communion with God at all times, you will stop looking for answers outside yourself. And you will stop giving answers when others come to you asking advice.

The only advice you can give to the seeker is this: seek for truth within your own heart, for there alone can you find it.

Share your experience? Yes, to be sure! Your story can be of immense help to others. But the boundaries of such an offering are clear. It is YOUR experience you are offering, a story, not a prescription for others. Whatever truth someone else sees in it is the truth he is meant to receive. And this, of course, will be different for each person who hears your story.

Ultimately, you alone are responsible for the beliefs you accept. Someone can tell you terrible lies, but it will never be his responsibility that you believed them. So do not waste your time blaming the guru, the cult or the church. Thank them instead. Tell them how grateful you are to them for pointing you on the true path. Without seeing their weakness and human frailty, you would have continued to idolize them and give your power away. Now you can reclaim your power and resume your path to peace.

Whether they realized it or not, they have done you a great service. Any abuser is a great teacher. He or she teaches you clearly what you are to avoid. Indeed, negative and positive teachings go hand in hand in building the character of the seeker.

To be abused and know it is a blessing. If you doubt this, think of the ones who sit in mesmerized bliss idolizing a teacher who takes their money, their sexual favors and their power and be thankful you have awakened from that kind of sleep.

Everybody at one time or another gives his power away, only to learn to take it back. That is an important and profound lesson on the spiritual path. Be grateful if you have learned this lesson. It means you are closer to your own truth, and if you are closer to your own truth, you are closer to God, the universal truth.

We come to oneness not through conformity, but through authenticity. When each being has the courage to be himself, he finds the highest truth he is capable of receiving. Finding the highest in himself, he merges easily with others. Yet his surrender to the common good does not come through self-violation, but through the transcendence of the pain of separation. In accepting his highest good, he also accepts yours. Indeed they are not separate.

How different this is from capitulation to authority, the subjugation of one ego to another. That is not the ending of suffering, but the beginning of it. Those who hold hostages must house and feed them. They must build many prisons. They will not find freedom, for they do not give it.

Freedom comes to the self when one rejects all forms of external authority and when one refuses to be an authority for anyone else. Paradoxically, that is also the moment in which the self becomes Self.

I urge you to claim what is yours. Empower yourself. Empower others. Be a brother, a sister, a friend, but accept no other teacher than the one who lives inside your heart.

Dissolving the Last Separation

Finding your true inner authority is a lifetime process. But what exactly is the authority that lies within the depths of your heart?

Clearly, that authority does not submit to the wants and needs of other people, however cleverly disguised. Nor does it submit to your own wants and needs, which are inevitably perceived in fear. The true authority of your heart blesses you and knows that you are completely loved and completely safe. It does not want. It does not need. It does not seek approval from others.

True authority is rock solid and self-nurtured. It moves perpetually toward its greatest joy without harming others. It knows without hesitation that its joy is not at odds with the joy of others. It serves others not out of sacrifice but through the extension of an inner joy that is constantly bubbling up and spilling over. It is totally committed to its own truth and totally welcoming of others. It seeks not to convert others to its own experience, nor to push them away. It merely rests in its experience, content, full, willing to share.

Yes, there is that rock solid conviction in you. You may not know how to access it, but it is there as surely as you are there. The question is "How can I be in communion with that wholesome self in me which is not in fear?"

The first step is: you must see what it is not.

It is not the desire to please others and obtain their approval, nor is it the desire to please self at the expense of others. It is deeper than all that.

It is that which lies behind all the gestures of fear, that

which abides in the silence, breathing deeply. That which lives beyond the restless turnings of the mind. That which is not drawn outward into other people's dramas, or inward into personal wants and needs.

Call it God. Call it your higher self. Call it your Christ Mind or your Buddha mind. Names do not matter.

You access this mind not in seeking, in doing, or in thinking. You access it through your own stillness, through your quiet acceptance of yourself and others, through your profound willingness to be present. You sink through the superficial dichotomies of mind into the depths of the heart.

And there, not surprisingly, you meet God not as Other, but as Self. In the silence, there is just a single heartbeat. It cannot belong to anyone else, for there is no one else there.

You see, if you were not already living in God's heart, you could not find your way there. Yet you do. Each of you, in some moment, stumbles on your absolute atonement and bliss. It comes so quickly you wonder if it was real. But, in fact, it was always real, always present, always awaiting your visitation, your openness of mind and heart.

Sit for a moment in profound forgiveness of yourself and everything in your experience and you will dissolve the walls which appear to hold you apart from God's grace. Moving into that grace, you leave all human conflict behind. The world as you know it disappears with your judgments of it. This is revelation. It is parting of the veil.

Do not make the mistake of thinking that this experience happens only to the chosen few. It happens to everyone. It is your destiny. You will awaken, because you cannot sleep forever. You cannot be in resistance forever. You cannot be in pain forever.

Sooner or later there is a letting go of resistance and withdrawal. There is no place to defend and nowhere to hide. You become visible. You become vulnerable. You stop reacting. You stop defending yourself or running away from the trespass of others. You can do this because you have stopped attacking them, both in overt and subtle ways. You stop withholding your love. You stop pushing their love away.

When your attack stops, you no longer fear retribution, so you can stand there naked, defenseless, simply as you are. You can be in your experience without defending it. You can accept the experience of others without judging it or trying to change it.

What is this? It is the birth of the Christ consciousness within you.

It is your resurrection. It is your internalization of the divine, the indwelling Spirit of God come to rest in your heart. Now you and He are not separate but are One person.

You talk about the trinity, but you do not understand it. Who is the Holy Spirit but the indwelling Christ, the Spirit of God that dwells in the heart of the Son. And who is the Son? Is it me, you, or both of us?

I will tell you this plainly. You will not get out of here alive as a human being. The human must die that the divine be born. Not because it is bad. But because it is the shell that holds the spirit, the cocoon that holds the wings of the butterfly.

But you do not have to wait until the moment of your physical death for the human to die. The human can die into the divine right now if you are willing to step into your divinity. If you are willing to stop playing the victim. If you are willing to stop resisting, defending, hiding, projecting shame and blame.

You cannot fly until you are willing to claim your wings. But once you do, you cannot remain in the dark shadows of your fear.

It is your choice. How would you choose? What would you be: victim or angel?

There is nothing in between! That which appears to exist in between is just the human shell. The being who has not yet chosen. The caterpillar dreaming of wings.

Salvation

You alone are the Christ, the Messiah, the one who brings salvation. For you are the only one who can step into your experience, own it fully, and lift it up. You are the one who brings the love you have sought from others. You are the one who rescues you from self-violation and abusive relationships.

When you feel powerless, when you feel like a victim, when your entire experience seems ego-driven, it is helpful to see the source of power outside your ego structures. Surrender to God without is certainly better than surrender to victimhood and powerlessness within. But the danger of surrender to God without is that you do not give up your victimhood. You still think that life is being "done" to you. The only difference is that now "God" is your ally.

If God is your ally, He can still become your enemy. You are still setting yourself up for betrayal.

Only when you know that you are the light bearer does the darkness disappear. But before you can become the lightbearer you must walk through your own darkness. The bearer of the light does not deny the darkness. He walks through it.

When there is nothing about yourself or anyone else that you are afraid to look at, the darkness has no more hold over you. Then you can walk through the darkness and be the light.

To pretend to be the lightbearer before you have faced your own fear is to be a pretender, an unhealed healer, a sham. All unhealed healers eventually come off their imaginary pedestals. Where there is only the pretension to light, the darkness still prevails.

To be the light you must embrace the darkness. Your darkness. Everyone's darkness. You must come to terms with the ego mind and see its absolute futility. You must learn to look at fear with love in your heart. Your fear. Your sister's fears. The rapist and murderer's fears.

You must know that all fear is alike and all fear betrays a lack of love. And you must learn to answer with love. Love is the answer to your deepest sense of separation. Not someone else's love. Your love for yourself. That is the light. That is the beginning of your bearing of the light.

Once you take the torch of truth up for yourself and bring love to the wounded parts of your mind, you take back your power. You surrender your victimhood. You can no longer be unfairly treated because you are the very source of love, acceptance, forgiveness.

Where does love come from? It comes from you. You are the way, the truth, and the life, just as I was. Don't look for the divine outside yourself, for it is discovered within. In your blessing of yourself is the entire world forgiven and blessed.

Look no further, brother and sister. It all begins with you. It ends with you. You are it. You are It!

Jerusalem

When does the kingdom of Heaven come to Earth? As soon as you accept the light, own it and become it. As soon as you are willing to open your heart and walk through your fears. As soon as you are willing to see yourself reflected in your brother's eyes.

When does the Messiah come? No, not later, not even at the end of time. But now. Now is the end of time. The end of separation. Now is the end of self-crucifixion. The end of projection. The final death knell of fear. Now.

Do not place salvation in the future or it will never come. Ask for it now. Accept it now.

God's kingdom manifests in this moment only. In this place only.

It does not require a special time. Every time is special. It does not require a special place. Every place is special.

When does Heaven come? When this moment is

enough. When this place is enough. When this friend is enough. When these events and circumstances are acceptable. When you no longer crave something other than what stands before you in this moment.

When you come to peace with what is, it dwells within you. There is no more separation. No more wanting. No more striving. No more resisting. No more withdrawal.

You are what is and it is you. You inhabit the cosmic body even as you move your physical arms and feet. You are freedom manifest in bodily form.

Even if you have a physical illness or disability. Even if you appear to suffer. There is no resentment. There is no presumption of attack. There is no guilt or perception of punishment. There is just the experience and your simple acceptance of it. There is just your innocence, however ungainly or compromised your position may look.

You cannot be compromised if you are in acceptance of your life. You cannot be resentful or wracked by grievances. Whatever your life is becomes the vehicle. Whatever the body looks like is acceptable. Whatever gifts you have to give are the perfect ones. It does not matter if they are not the ones you thought you would have or the ones you wanted.

When you are in acceptance of your life, you do not refuse to give your gifts because they do not meet your expectations. You give them because they are there to be given. Because the opportunity to give presents itself. And in the giving of those gifts, your destiny is revealed.

Only the God within you knows why your outer life looks a certain way. She knows but she cannot tell you, because you would not understand. But when you begin to trust the gifts that have been given you, the purpose of your life becomes clear. You understand. You may not be able to put it into words, but you understand. You see how every lesson, every constriction, every problem, every moment of suffering was absolutely necessary for the gift to be revealed. For the gift to be trusted. For the gift to be given and received.

When you are in acceptance of your life, you are profoundly grateful, because you see and feel that a greater intelligence is operating in your life. That intelligence rests inside your heart and the heart of all beings. Its serves your good and the good of others simultaneously. It honors all.

Faith

Y ou cannot have faith in God unless you have faith in yourself and your brother. But ask yourself "What is faith?"

Is it the belief in something that you perceive is lacking in your life? If so, it is not faith. Faith is never the perception of lack.

Faith is the perception of goodness in that which appears to be evil. It is the perception of abundance in what appears to be not enough. It is the perception of justice in that which seems unfair.

Faith is the bringing of love to the unlovable. It is the bringing of compassion to the unmerciful. It is the bringing of God's presence to the places where She seems to be absent.

Faith is the recognition of a higher good, a higher order, a higher truth than the one the frightened child would see. And faith is always won in the trenches.

Where do you find your faith? In your most intense suffering!

Where do you find God's presence? In the moments when you feel totally abandoned and rejected!

This seems to be unfair. But it is hardly so. As long as you believe that you can be attacked, the Christ child will be perceived as an abused child.

Small and defenseless, he does not fight back. He does not resist evil, because he knows evil is simply the perceived absence of love. And the perceived absence of love can be transformed only by love's presence.

The strongest power in the universe seems to be so weak, so easily overpowered, crucified and forgotten. But it is not so. All who attack the Christ must return to serve Him. And they will keep coming back until they learn that He is them. And therefore He cannot be destroyed.

Is this unfair? To know that all attack is self-attack. To fulfill the karmic law until one learns to rise above it.

How can it be unfair?

Only in the deepest pain of existence is faith in God discovered and confirmed. This is no mystery. It is the turning away from self attack. It is the moment in which you realize that everything outside you is merely a reflection of an attitude you have toward yourself.

In that moment, you stop being a victim.

In that moment, you know your life has been perfect just as it is and has been.

In that moment, you claim your life, your authorship, your divine lineage. You are not the boy who was nailed to the cross or the girl burned at the stake, but the child who learned to bless himself and in so doing saved the world.

You are the saint. The angel. The savior.

When you awaken, my job will be complete.

In truth, it is already complete. But you will keep returning until you know this in your heart, once and for all.

False Prophets, The Devil and the Antichrist

A false prophet is one who makes his ego into a god. He claims to be self-realized, free of suffering and fear, but sooner or later his behavior betrays him and he is exposed as an imposter. I have said before and I will say again: "By your fruits, you will know them." Do not listen to the clever, persuasive words of those who claim spiritual authority. Look to their actions. See if what they do is at odds with what they say.

If you are wise, you will not follow anyone. Then you will not be misled. But if you must find a teacher or a leader, look for one who empowers you to hear the truth in your own heart. Look for one who loves you without seeking to control you, one who is able to tell you his or her truth without expecting you to agree with it. Find a teacher who honors you and treats you with dignity and respect.

By their fruits you will know them.

Anyone who claims a special knowledge and sells it for a price is a false prophet. Anyone who needs you to bow down, agree with his opinions, or carry out his agenda is a false prophet. Anyone who asks for your money or sexual favors is a false prophet. Anyone who encourages you to give away your power, your self-respect or your dignity is a false prophet. Do not abide with such people. They do not have your good at heart. They do not even have their own good at heart. They are still abusing themselves and others.

Do not seek the company of one who smothers you and does not give you the freedom to be yourself. Do not accept a teacher who tries to make decisions for you. Do not accept the teachings or the friendship of one who criticizes you or blames you for his problems. Do not let anyone dictate to you or control your life.

Neither dictate to someone else. Any need you have to control another person or make decisions for that person is abusive. Do not trespass on others or seek to take away their freedom to decide what they they want. Any attempt to do so simply binds you to the wheel of suffering.

What you give to others is what you get back. Do not be a victimizer or a victim. Be yourself and allow others to be themselves.

The Antichrist seeks salvation and peace by controlling others. It is the attempt to force reconciliation. It never works. What lives by the sword dies by the sword. Wrong means always lead to wrong ends.

However, even the Antichrist is not evil. He is simply starved for love. Being starved by love, he tries to buy it, demand it, control it. And by so doing he pushes love further away. The more love eludes him the more vicious he gets. His fear begets the fear of others.

Often the Antichrist impersonates the Christ. The wolf appears in sheep's clothing. She seems to be gentle, compassionate and wise, but it is all an act. As soon as she has your allegiance, her true colors appear. That is why you must be very careful. You think you are worshipping Christ, but it is not Christ you are worshipping. It is the Devil in disguise.

What is the devil? It is simply the ego mind. The scared, unhappy, angry little kid inside of you who feels unfairly treated. That's the only devil. And it lives in every one of you, because every one of you beat up mercilessly upon yourselves. Each of you has a very wounded child inside of you. That's the only devil.

Don't try to make the devil powerful. He is only formidable because you resist him. Don't push him away anymore. Take him in your arms and rock him. Hold him, speak gently to him. Love him as your own precious child. For He is. He is the Christ child asleep in your arms. When he knows he is lovable, he will not plot to betray you. All his shenanigans stem from the belief he has that he is not lovable.

When you have embraced the wounded child within, his angelic presence is revealed. Lucifer is not a confused human, but a fallen angel. In your love, his fall is broken and he finds his wings. In his redemption is yours guaranteed.

Lucifer means light bearer. He is the wounded child transformed into the risen Christ. The angelic presence leading the human into God's eternal embrace.

Until you know that love can neither be demanded nor withheld, you cannot give and receive it without conditions. The Antichrist impersonates devil and savior in his empty search for man's allegiance and love. In the end, he gives up. In great sorrow, he knows he cannot win. He thinks he is done for. He awaits God's wrath.

But, surprisingly, it does not come. Instead, God approaches him and lifts him up into his arms. "Welcome home, Lucifer," he says. "Welcome Home."

And so Lucifer regains his place in heaven. And, through him, man is tested in the fire of perceived inequality and abuse. When Lucifer is redeemed, the light comes to man. Victim and victimizer meet face to face. Equality and justice are realized.

Then Antichrist's work on earth is done. The long detour is over. We are beyond temptation, for we have taken the journey into fear and back. And we remember what we saw and how it did not bring us either happiness or peace. We remember.

Dark Wings to Light

The greatest block to spiritual awakening is the pretension that there is no suffering in your life, that you have no pain. If you don't feel pain in your life, you are either awakened or you are in denial.

I hate to burst your bubble, but I must tell you there are very few awakened beings on the planet and chances are you are not among them. I say this so that you can be realistic about your spiritual life.

Even though you have dulled the pain, being frozen in fear is hardly spiritual. Indeed, all psycho-emotional defenses you have built to protect yourself are just blocks to love's presence. True, you built them to deter or withstand abuse, but they also deter love. They push love away. They close down your heart.

You see, you cannot awaken with a closed heart. The first step in the process of awakening is always "open your heart." As soon as the heart is open, you will feel all the pain and shame you have intellectualized or repressed. It is inevitable.

Let it come. Let the pain come forth so that you may be

cleansed and purified. If you continue to live with the pain, you will live a terribly limited life. Profound, seemingly overwhelming fears will move unconsciously in your psyche, preventing you from experiencing your true self or from opening up to genuine intimacy with others.

Let the pain come up. Let the heart be open. In feeling the pain, you begin to work it through. You see that it is not overwhelming. You see you can be with it without being destroyed. Feel the hurt, the anger, and the betrayal you never allowed yourself to feel as a child, or even as an adult. Let the repressed sense of violation come to the surface. You cannot cease being a victim until you get in touch with why you became one in the first place.

Get in touch with why you feel betrayed. Get in touch with the judgments you make about yourself. Go deeper and deeper until you see the self-betrayal and own it. No, don't beat yourself for it. Just gently own it and grieve it fully.

It is a spiritual law that no one can betray you but you. Don't settle for the victim role. It keeps you from experiencing all the pain of your self-betrayal. Let it all come up. Let the pain be released. Let the self judgment and attack be released. You have carried all this too long.

Very few people have done their own healing process. Even the ones who are out there trying to help others. Most of them too have not healed from within. They have not owned their own victim drama. How can they help you?

Others cannot help you. You must do this healing for yourself. If you need a coach, choose one who has traveled the road him or herself. And be careful; there are not many who have. If you look carefully, you can see if the darkness in them has been integrated or if they are still pushing it away.

Anyone who is afraid of his own darkness cannot move toward the light. Anyone who rejects his humanness and pretends to be completely of spirit is unintegrated and unwhole. Do not accept a wounded healer, even if he has an angelic name. Even if others think highly of him.

Find a coach with no agenda. One who can say: "Yes. I

have been there. I know something of the terrain, but I do not know specifically what will happen for you. All I can do is accompany you, empower you to go deeply into the shadows, and see what happens. All I can do is be the 'friend,' not the expert."

No one is the expert. There are simply those who have made the journey and those who have not. The former do not claim professional status. They have been humbled by their own journey. The latter make great claims, which shatter the first time they identify with you and their own buttons get pushed.

One who has made the journey to hell and back does not have sky fever. She is not of the fairy realm. She smells of fire and earth. She has undulations on her brow from centuries of occupation by water. Her beauty is of the earth. She is a weathered princess, a mother, not a virginal bride.

To resurrect, to rise into the sky, you must first meet the devil head on. If you keep looking for him in others, you will not find him. If you don't believe in him, you haven't bothered to look inside your own mind.

The devil is your own angelic presence defiled. It is all of your forgetting, all of your self-violation. It is the wounded one, the crucified one, the angel who has fallen from the sky into the muck, into the savage pull of worldly incarnation. He is you more than your fairy self is. Your fairy self is as thin as air. It is not of the earth. It cannot rise from that which it has never encountered.

The devil is of earth. Your ego mind is the creator of earth with all its manifest pain and beauty. Do not reject your creation before you have come to know it. Walk in the rain. Roast in the sun. Roll in the mud. Taste it fully. Do not try to leave the world before you are ready.

The urge to leave is the final addiction to pain. I must tell you frankly there is no place to go. This is it. You cannot move outside your own creation. You must move in it, be with it, and learn how to shift it.

God will not come as a savior to free you from a world

of your own making. That is an old paradigm solution. It does not empower you. Even if it were possible, it would not be in your best interest.

God comes through your own gesture of acceptance toward your ego mind. He comes in the love and compassion you bring to the wounded one within and without. He comes when you reach down to embrace the dark wings that hover in front of the door of your fear.

These wings will not hurt you. No one is defiled no matter how great the hurt. No one is robbed of his or her innocence, no matter how much abuse has been given or received. See through the dark disguise and come into the warmth of these wings. There is a door here that leads straight to the heart. Come into your pain, sister.

You cannot come to God if you don't go through the dark night of the soul. All your fear and shame must be raised. All your feelings of separation must come up for healing. How can you rise from the ashes of your pain unless you will acknowledge the pain?

Those who pretend that the wound is not there never begin the spiritual journey. Those who open the wound and beat themselves or others with it do not move beyond the first step in the healing process.

If you want to heal, remember, let the pain come up. Acknowledge the wound. Be with it and let it teach you.

- Feel the pain. Remember the violation.
- Forgive yourself.
- Be kind to yourself.
- See the perpetrator's pain.
- See the attack as a call for love.
- Stand up for yourself now.
- Vow never to be a victim again.
- Vow never to betray yourself again.
- Understand you accepted pain because you wanted love and didn't know how to get it.

- Say what you want now.
- Say no to violation.
- Learn to say no to what you do not want.
- Learn to say yes to what you do want.
- Do not confuse the two.
- Do not accept what does not feel good.
- Tell the truth, even if it means that others leave.
- Be firm. Be clear. Get on with your life.
- Be willing to feel your feelings and to let others know how you feel. Own what you feel and don't make others responsible for it. There is no blame appropriate here, for you or anyone else.
- Know that healing is a life-long process. There are more and more layers of abandonment that will come up. It is okay. Now you know you can feel the pain and move through it. Now you can have confidence in your healing journey.
- You need not go looking for the darkness. It will come to you all by itself. Once you are willing to heal, the pain of the broken self automatically comes up. Fragments of the puzzle surface and the picture becomes clear. This doesn't happen all at once.
- Be patient. You can't rush the process. Your healing has its own gentle pace. Stay with it. Don't push too hard or you will go back into fear and freeze up. Just be willing to deal with each issue in the present moment.

This is what the spiritual path is all about. Healing our wounds. Healing our private pain by making it public. Confessing our shame. Finding our healing partners.

This is not work that can be done in a mountain cave. Withdrawal from life simply deadens the senses. It is neither advantageous or necessary.

The shortest path to enlightenment is the one that moves directly through our hearts. Through our relationships. Through our pain and our grief and our fear. It seems not to be a path of dignity, yet it is the most dignified path of all. In it dark wings become illumined and the darkness begets its own healing power. For, in the darkness, we are nurtured and prepared. From that dark womb we go forward toward the light. Without it, we would not be born.

Without it, we cannot be born again.

Uncreating the Wound

Understand that, if you did not make the wound, you could not unmake it. So be glad that your suffering is no one else's fault. Celebrate the fact that redemption is possible, that you can undo what you have done. But do not beat yourself with the knowledge that you are the creator of your suffering. Your creations happen unconsciously, so in truth you do not know what you are doing. If you knew, you wouldn't do it.

You do it because you don't know and you need to know. Becoming conscious of the way in which we abuse ourselves or give others permission to abuse us is essential to undoing the abuse.

Until you become aware of the dynamic, you cannot change it. Therefore you are not responsible for it. You can never be held responsible for what you do not understand. Your responsibility begins with your awareness of the abuse.

Pain is the ultimate tool of awareness. Until you feel the pain, you don't know any violation has taken place. Once you become aware of the violation, your journey to healing begins.

So any pain you feel is not bad. It is not a punishment. It is a call to become conscious, to raise the hidden suffering into awareness.

Don't beat yourself with the knowledge that you made a mistake, that you acted unconsciously, irresponsibly.

87

Instead, embrace the correction. Atone consciously for the mistake. Take responsibility for your behavior so that the mistake, the pain of self-violation, and the pattern of abuse surrounding it can be undone.

Pain is a call to consciousness. Do not treat the call with recipes that would deaden it and leave your deeper suffering and dis-ease untouched. Treat the cause of the pain: the unhappiness, the suicidal self hatred, the self-violation.

The treatment for all types of separation is simply acceptance and love. Start by accepting the pain and asking it to take you to its cause. Start by admitting your mistakes without beating yourself for them. Start by accepting your feelings, whatever they are. Start by bringing love to yourself.

Become aware of the self-violation, forgive yourself for it, and bring love to the wound. This is the recipe for healing. It is not a complicated or difficult process unless you refuse to own it.

Healing the wound ultimately means undoing its cause. It means understanding what self-depreciation brought the abuse in. Once that understanding is there and love is given in answer to it, the cause of the wound is neutralized and no further abusive situations will be created.

Until that understanding dawns and that responsibility is taken, new potentially abusive situations will be continually created. Each of them conspires to wake you up. None of them carries the necessity of pain if you are a willing learner.

Each learning relationship offers you the opportunity to say no to what does not honor you. If you can say no before the violation comes, you can avoid additional suffering. Saying no to another person, of course, implies an awareness that you have tended to say "yes" in the past. That means that you are owning the dynamic. You know you create abuse by accepting conditional love. You create abuse by saying yes to self-degradation in exchange for the security and approval you want. You say yes to fear by bargaining for love.

Now you know it will not work. Love cannot be bargained for. You must wait for the real thing. You must reject all the deals that are offered to you. Each one is a form of attack.

When love is given to you without conditions you will know it. You cannot mistake it, because it honors you totally. It doesn't ask from you more than you can give. It doesn't manipulate or demand. It accepts you as you are and blesses you.

If you do not know how to create this blessing for yourself, how can you receive it from another? Practice it. Practice accepting yourself just as you are. Then you will know what love is and you will recognize it when it comes into your life.

If you love yourself conditionally, you will draw others into your life who do the same. You cannot receive from others what you are unable to give to yourself.

So you have plenty of work to do. Inner work. Inner acceptance. As the inner healing is done, the outer life begins to reflect it. Those who are drawn in are more respectful and supportive. There is less struggle, more grace. The heart opens gently and peace unfolds.

Love's Presence

When God is standing securely in your life, there is harmony within and peace without. You honor yourself and other's equally. That is the sign of God's grace.

This grace then becomes the guiding light of your life. It is the compass by which you navigate. Whenever you experience disharmony within or contention without, you know you have lost your alignment with the divine Will. You know it is time to stop, breathe, and re-center. It is time to surrender your personal concepts and desires and pray for the highest good of all concerned.

Grace is not continuous for anyone. New lessons

emerge that must be learned. No matter how far the heart has opened, there will be times when it still contracts in fear. That is to be expected.

Perfection does not happen externally. As long as you are here in a body you cannot be mistake free.

So you begin to understand that grace comes and goes. Alignment happens and is lost. But only temporarily. Because you know how to re-establish the connection. You know how to re-enter the dance.

The rhythm of the dance beats with each heart. The breath comes in and goes out. God appears and disappears. Attention comes and goes. Self is forgotten and remembered. There is alternation, a movement to and fro, yet also an overall continuity into which moments of discontinuity are welcomed. It is a gentle, forgiving dance, not a rigid one.

This is the best life has to offer. If you are looking for more than this, you search in vain. If you are looking for absolute enlightenment, absolute certainty, you will not find it.

Grace happens in the flow of life, not apart from it. And life is like a river moving from the mountains toward the sea. When it leaves the mountains, it rushes downward, impetuous and intent to reach its goal. Then it levels out and moves for what seems like an eternity through fields and plains, separating into different streams, joining with other bodies of water. By the time it reaches the ocean, it no longer has any urgency. Instead, it has a confidence born of experience. By the time it reaches the ocean, it no longer sees itself as anything other than ocean. It rests completely in itself, without beginning or end.

It will be that way with you too. When you enter fully into your life, all that held you separate will be gently washed away. Breathing in, you will open to embrace what comes. Breathing out, you will gently release it.

Part 4

Right
Livelihood

The Gifts of God

The gifts you have been given in this life do not belong to you alone. They belong to everyone. Do not be selfish and withhold them. Do not be selfish and imprison yourself in a lifestyle that holds your spirit hostage and provides no spontaneity or grace in your life.

Risk being yourself fully.

Let go of the expectations others have for you. Let go of all the "shoulds" and "have tos" and consider what thoughts and actions bring you the greatest joy. Live from the inside out, not from the outside in.

To move toward your joy is not selfish. It is in fact the most kind action you can perform toward others. That is because your gift is needed. The spirit of others cannot be lifted up unless you trust your gift and give it unconditionally to the world.

Consider how empty life would be if others around you chose to abandon their gifts. All that you find wonderful in life — the music, the poetry, the films, the sports, the laughter — would vanish if others withheld their gifts from you.

Do not withhold your gift from others. Do not make the mistake of thinking that you have no gift to give. Everyone has a gift. But don't compare your gift to the gifts of others, or you may not value it sufficiently.

Your gift brings joy to yourself and joy to others. If there is no joy in your life, it is because you are withholding your gift. You are not trusting it. You are not actively bringing the gift forward into manifestation in your life.

All gifts are creative expressions of self. They reveal the self. They break down the barriers of separation and allow others to know who you are.

To create is to bring an inner awareness into form. That awareness does not exist in the world in the way *you* would express it. Your expression of it is unique, authentic. It is fresh, honest, manifested out of your own experience.

A creative person does not take direction from the outside.

She does not imitate established forms. She listens within.

Now she may survey the world. She may even study and scrutinize it. But then she internalizes what she sees. She takes it in and digests it. She considers it in the light of her own experience. She feels it. She owns it. She makes it hers. And then she gives it back. And what she gives back is her vision. Her unique perspective. Her story.

And if she is honest, others will respond to her, because they hear their story in hers. They will share her vision, for a moment, for a day, for a week or even longer. Others will support her creative work. And their support will make it easier for her. The energy that she puts out will begin to come back to her. She will feel appreciated emotionally and financially. It is a beautiful process.

Perhaps you have tried this and it hasn't come to fruition. Perhaps you are still struggling to manifest your gift. "What am I doing wrong?" you ask. "Why isn't the universe supporting me?"

The answer is a simple one. Either what you are trying to manifest isn't your gift or you don't believe in your gift sufficiently.

"Well, how do I know?" you inquire.

Ask yourself "Am I doing this because it brings me great joy or because I am seeking the approval of others?" If your action is not joyful, it will not bring happiness to yourself or others. You may succeed or you may fail, but happiness will be missing. Only that which comes from your heart with great enthusiasm will prosper on all levels. Only that which you love will touch others and bring true appreciation your way.

Appreciation and approval are two entirely different things. Appreciation is the natural, spontaneous flow of energy back to you when others feel connected to you and your story. There is nothing you can do to precipitate appreciation other than to be yourself and tell the truth. You simply cannot be in control of what comes back. When you have shared authentically, something essential always comes back. It may not look like what you expect, because what your ego is looking for is not appreciation, but approval.

The search for approval is based on the consciousness that you are not enough. You want others to give you the love that feels missing in your life. This search is a futile one. If you feel empty and seek to be filled from the outside, others will feel attacked. They will experience your request for appreciation as a demand. They will be repelled or repulsed. And then you will feel even more empty, rejected, abused.

Energy cannot return to you unless and until you put energy out. Putting out a demand is not putting out energy. It is putting out a vacuum that sucks other people's energy. It shouts out to the world "I need you to value me because I don't value myself." Unless and until you love and appreciate yourself, other people won't receive your gift no matter how hard you try to give it to them.

Putting out energy means taking yourself seriously, but not too seriously. It means valuing yourself enough to be willing to share with others. It does not mean attacking people with your gifts. When you have a lot of expectations about how people should receive your gifts, you make it impossible for them to receive them.

If you value your gift, it won't matter so much how others respond to it. Even if they don't give you positive feedback, you won't be dissuaded from offering your gift again and again.

Happiness and personal fulfillment flow from the commitment you make to yourself. This commitment will be tested again and again. Over and over, you will be asked by the universe to offer your gift in the face of criticism, skepticism or apparent lack of appreciation. And each time rejection comes, you will be faced with the decision "Do I do this again?"

If the gift is false, sooner or later you will stop offering it. It will become apparent to you that you never receive what you want to receive when you offer your services. It will become clear that offering these services is a way of beating yourself up. So you will stop attacking yourself by offering a gift that is not yours to offer.

On the other hand, if the gift is true, you will learn from apparent failure and rejection. You will learn to value the gift more deeply and to offer it more authentically. You will gradually stop attacking people with your gift and start creating a more loving space in which the gift can be offered and received.

An authentic gift will develop as you trust it. A false gift will not. The former is the gift of Spirit and it is your responsibility to nurture it into existence. The latter is the expectation of your ego, which sooner of later must be surrendered if your true gifts are to emerge.

One is the bringer of appreciation, which deepens intimacy and connection with others. The other brings approval or rejection, both of which bring isolation, pain and humiliation.

So ask yourself "Am I seeking approval? Am I looking for strokes I am unwilling to give to myself? Do I love and value myself right now or am I looking for love to come from others so that I know that I am really okay?"

Ask yourself "Am I trusting my gift sufficiently?" Am I underconfident and hiding my light or am I overconfident and attacking other people with my gift?"

Honest answers to these questions will dissolve any confusion you have about this issue.

Nurturing the Gift

Many people say they don't know what their gifts are, but this is just denial. You can't be conscious and not know what your gift is. Your gift always lies where your joy and enthusiasm run deepest.

The only difficulty you will have in recognizing your gift is that it may not fit your pictures of what a gift is supposed to be. Suppose, for example, you have excellent listening skills. People come to you with their life dramas and leave happier and more peaceful. Over and over again, others tell you they like being around you. They feel that you accept them as they are. They feel empowered by you. You don't seem to take on their problems. And your presence has an uplifting effect on people.

But you don't get it. You don't do anything in particular, so you can't understand there is a gift involved here. You keep looking for the gift outside of your experience. You think: "Maybe I should go back to school and be a librarian?" But you already have two masters degrees. You've already had all the training you need. Training is not the issue. Changing careers is not the issue.

The issue is that the gift is staring you in the face and you refuse to see it. You think the gift is "a doing," but it's not. The gift is "a way of being" that is effortless and exultant. It comes naturally to you. It immediately and palpably brings joy to others.

"Well," you think, "maybe I should go back to school and get a degree in counseling. Nobody will want to come to me and pay me money unless I have a degree." But you miss the point. It doesn't matter what you do. We are not talking about a doing, but a way of being. Whatever you do, you can express your gift. You don't need a special role, a special platform.

Seeking a special role is a way of pushing the gift away. It's saying: "This gift doesn't really meet my expectations. It can't support me. Why can't I have a real gift. Others do. What's wrong with me?"

If you could take the same unconditional love and acceptance that you offer to others and offer it to yourself, you would turn your entire life around, because you would begin trusting the gift yourself. Until you value and trust the gift, how can the universe support you?

Many of your gifts go unacknowledged because they don't match your pictures of what a gift should be. Or you devalue the gift and push it away by comparing it to that of others. You envy their gift. You would rather have theirs than your own. What a foolish waste of time and energy!

Come on, friends, get on with it! Embrace the gift you have been given, no matter what it looks like. You'll see. It will be fun. Others will enjoy it. Life will begin to flow as the gift is offered without expectation of return.

Every time you place a condition on your willingness to offer the gift, you push it further away. "I will sing only if I have an audience of 1,000 people and I make at least $5,000!" Supposing not that many people have heard of you, how many offers to sing are going to come your way?

More procrastination. More resistance. More sacrifice and self-torture! How is your lifework to evolve if you do not take the first step to bring it into existence?

You lifework is like a baby. It needs to be nurtured both in and out of the womb. When you first become aware of what your gift is, don't go around announcing it to the rooftops. Keep your own counsel. Begin singing in the shower. Find a teacher. Practice every day.

Then when your gift is ready to be shared with others, find an informal, low-key environment that does not put a lot of pressure on you to perform or on others to respond. Be easy with it, the way you would be if a child wanted to share a song. Be that child. No matter how anxious you are to grow up with your gift, you must take the time to be the child first.

Learn, grow, and let your gift be nurtured into manifestation. Take small risks, then bigger ones. Sing to small audiences and gain your confidence. Then, without your doing anything, the audiences will grow.

Those who refuse to start small never accomplish anything. They shoot for the moon and never learn to stand on the earth.

Don't be afraid to be an apprentice. If you admire someone who has a gift that resembles yours, don't be afraid to ask for lessons. That is one of the ways you learn to trust the gift.

On the other hand, you can't be a student forever. There

comes a time when the student is ready to leave the teacher behind. When that moment comes, step forward. Trust the gift. Trust all the hours you have practiced. Step forth. Have faith in yourself. You are ready.

The way you relate to your gift says a lot about whether you are happy or not. Happy people are expressing their gifts all their time, on whatever level and in whatever arena life offers them. Unhappy people are holding onto their gifts until life gives them the perfect venue.

I can tell you now, the perfect venue never comes. Even if life seems to match all of your pictures, when the moment comes you have been waiting for, it looks nothing like you expected it to.

It's quite simple, really. All your pictures have to go. Part of trusting the gift is letting go of the way you think the gift should be received. That is not your affair. It is none of your business. No matter how great you become, you will never know who will be touched by your work and who will turn away.

To give the gift, you must release it. You must not be attached to who receives it and who doesn't. Nobody speaks to everyone. Some share their gifts with an audience of a few people. Some share with a few million. In the former case, the sharing is intimate and deep. In the latter, it is superficial and wide.

It is not for you to judge.

Don't judge the gift. Embrace it, value it and give it. And don't judge the way it is received. Give it without attachment to results, without expectations of return.

You can't hold onto your gift and give it away at the same time. When you see the absurdity of trying to do this, you will give your gift the wings it deserves. And that is the moment when your gift will reach those who are reaching out for it. And the energy of it will move through them and back to you. The cycle of giving and receiving will be complete. Appreciation will be felt, and a new cycle of giving will begin.

Commitment to Self & Others

Your commitment to the expression of your gift will transform your life. All the structures in your life which hold you in limitation begin to fall apart as soon as you make this inner commitment to yourself. Trying to change these structures from the outside in is futile. That is not how change occurs.

Change occurs from the inside out. As you embrace your gift and move through your fear of expressing it, old, outdated lifestyle structures are deenergized. Without receiving new energy from you, these structures dissolve. You don't have to do anything. As they dissolve, they create a more open space within your own consciousness for the gift to be recognized, given and received.

Your work situation, your family life, your sleeping and eating patterns all begin to shift as you get about the business of honoring yourself and moving toward your joy. Without struggle, you unhook from roles and relationships that no longer serve your continued growth. This happens spontaneously. There is no forcing or violation involved.

When faced with your absolute, uncompromising commitment to yourself, others either join you or move swiftly out of your way. Grey spaces created by your ambivalence — your desire to have something and give it up at the same time — move toward yea or nay. Clarity emerges as the clouds of self-doubt and attachment are burned away by the committed, radiant self.

When one person moves toward individuation, it gives everyone permission to do the same. Dysfunctional family structures are dismantled and new structures that honor the individuals involved are put in their place.

This is what commitment to self does. It destroys sloppiness, co-dependency, neurotic bargaining for love, boredom, apathy and critical behavior. It frees the individuals to be themselves and to come back into a more genuine alignment in a conscious way.

One person's fidelity to self and willingness to live her dream explodes the entire edifice of fear that surrounds her. It is that simple. And it all happens as gently as the first "yes" said in the silence of the heart.

No one can be abandoned by your "yes" to yourself. If you think otherwise, you will build a prison of fear and guilt around you. Your "yes" to your essential self and life purpose is also a "yes" to the other person's essential self and purpose in life. Neurotic bargains for love in which boundaries are constantly compromised cannot stand in the light of self-affirmation. In setting yourself free, you call others to their freedom. Whether they answer the call, of course, is up to them.

The call to self-actualization is not a call to abandon others. It is not a call to separation or the avoidance of responsibility. The call to honor self is also a call to honor others. When one is not happy, usually others are not either. Sooner or later, this unhappiness must be confronted and discussed.

The call to self-actualization comes to fruition only to the extent that the heart remains open. It is not a shutting down, but an opening up.

Sometimes others cannot see the gift your self-commitment gives to them and you may have to act in a way that others cannot understand or support. That will be difficult for you, but don't capitulate to those who would make you feel guilty for following your heart. Stand firm with your commitment to yourself, but keep your heart open to the pain of others. Love them, bless them, talk with them, support them in any way that you can, but do not allow them to turn you from your responsibility to yourself.

Your commitment to other people must be an extension of your commitment to yourself, not at odds with it. How can you choose between your good and that of another? It is not possible.

No one asks you to make such a choice.

Somewhere there is a decision that honors you and also honors others. Find that decision. Be committed to finding it.

Don't abandon yourself. Don't abandon others. Rest in your commitment to self. Invite others into it. Rest in your commitment to others. Bring your whole self into it.

Be who you are and be willing to share. Don't dishonor yourself. Don't exclude others from your love. What else can you do? What else needs to be done?

Let the old form go. Let the new form of your life emerge at its own pace. Go willingly into the open space of "not knowing." Whenever you release the past, you must enter this space. Don't be afraid. Don't be embarrassed. It is okay not to know. It is okay to let things evolve.

Just be present and tell the truth. Be patient. Growing is a process. Be gentle with yourself and others. You will not do it without making mistakes.

The Only Work There Is

All spiritual work involves expressing the self joyously and uplifting others. If your work is not joyous, if it doesn't express your talents and abilities, and if it doesn't uplift others, it is not spiritual work. It is the world's work.

Many times I have asked you to be in the world but not of it. What does this mean?

It means that you can do the tasks that other men and women do, but you do them joyfully in the spirit of love. You give your labor as a gift. There is no sacrifice involved.

If there is sacrifice involved, there will be no joy. And so there will be no gift.

Do not work out of duty. Even if you serve others. Do what you do joyfully or do not do it.

Do not do something you don't enjoy just to earn money. Even if that money supports a family of people, they will not prosper through your sacrifice.

Nothing prospers that does not come from love.

There are hundreds, if not thousands of ways, in which you can cheat yourself and work out of sacrifice or duty. There are just as many ways in which you can cheat others and work out of impatience and greed. Be aware of the many subtle ways in which you can betray yourself and/or others. Do not settle for the rewards the world would give you. Material wealth, name and fame will not bring you happiness.

Only work that is joyful will bring you happiness. Only work that is joyful will bring happiness to others. Do not think that happiness can come from sacrifice or struggle. The means must be consistent with the ends. The goal unfolds through the process itself.

Be wary of work motivated by guilt or spiritual pride. Do not try to save yourself by helping others. Do not try to save others when it is you yourself who needs to be saved.

First, put things right in your own mind. Learn to forgive the past and honor yourself here and now. Learn to trust your gifts. When you are fully expressing who you are joyfully, your work will naturally extend to those who will benefit from it or from your personal example. This is God's work. It requires no marketing. It has an agenda of its own.

Having found your lifework, the greatest obstacle to its fulfillment lies in your attempt to "direct" it. You cannot make your spiritual work happen. If you try, you will fail. You will see the loftiest work be tainted by spiritual pride and undermined by your ego expectations.

You cannot do your spiritual work the same way you did your worldly work. The former requires surrender. The latter requires the illusion of control.

As soon as you give up the need to control, any work can become spiritual. As soon as you try to take charge, the most spiritual projects begin to fall apart.

What is spiritual is not what you do, but how you do it. What you do joyfully is spiritual work.

What is worldly is not what you do, but how you do it. What you do out of duty, sacrifice, or the search for approval is worldly work.

It is not the outer shell that matters, but the inner

motivation. It is not "what," but "how."

Do not try to discover your life purpose from the outside in. It is not possible.

Do not try to discover your life purpose by listening to the ideas and opinions of others. It is not possible.

You discover your life work by listening to the voice of your heart. There is no other way.

It seems to be a lonely journey and, in a way, it is, because no one else can do it for you. You must run the first few miles by yourself. You must demonstrate your commitment. You must show that you will not be drawn off-course by others.

In time, others come who share your path. This is inevitable. You do not have to go looking for them. You meet them in the natural course of honoring yourself and being open to your experience.

The Myth of Material Prosperity

Let's be clear that few people are committed to God's work. Of those who say they are, only a handful are actively demonstrating that commitment. Don't expect the world to support your journey to authenticity. It will not!

The world supports only what it understands. And right now all it understands is duty and sacrifice. That will change in time. But don't expect it too soon. Don't go into your lifework with the hope of worldly support and approval.

Those who understand my teachings and try to live them are often treated with disdain by the world. Don't be surprised if this happens to you. It is not a sign of divine disapproval that other men and women feel envious of or threatened by you.

If this happens, bear it patiently and send love and acceptance to others. When they see that you have their highest good at heart, they will soften to you. If you are committed to the journey, your patience will be rewarded.

But, if you are seeking approval or recognition, you will not find it.

Pay no mind to the religion of abundance. That is no more true nor helpful than the religion of sacrifice. God does not necessarily reward spiritual work with material success. All rewards are spiritual. Happiness, joy, compassion, peace, sensitivity: these are the rewards for a life lived in integrity.

If material success does not come, it is not important. If it seems important, and resentment develops, then more ego simply needs to be stripped away. One must learn, once and for all, to stop measuring spiritual riches with a worldly yardstick.

If material success comes, it is often a test to see if one can transcend self-interest and greed. One who is unwilling to share his material wealth with others is not spiritual.

Material wealth, like all other gifts, is given that it may be shared with others. If you are holding onto God's gift to you, you will not reap the reward of true prosperity, which is happiness and peace.

Don't make the mistake of thinking that your lifework must bring in a large paycheck. If you believe this, and your work does not meet with worldly success, you will think you have chosen the wrong work. You will feel inadequate and unworthy. You will beat yourself up and abandon your gift.

On the other hand, don't make the mistake of thinking that you must be poor to serve God. A rich person can serve God as well as one of humble means if he is willing to share his riches. It matters not how much you hold in your hands, but whether your hands are extended outward to your brother or sister. Look from the inside out, look into your heart, at your intention, and you will see things as God sees them.

All men and women are entrusted with a gift. It does not matter how one person's gift compares to that of another. What matters is that each person comes to embrace the gift and offer it to others.

Part 5

Healing
The Divided Self

Indulgence and Renunciation

Too many people still approach their lives with the expectation: "If I am good, God will reward me." Their understanding of abundance is one dimensional. They think they can manipulate God with the right mantra. When all their magical thinking fails, they feel like complete failures. If they get cancer or go bankrupt, they start to beat themselves up mercilessly. They give up all hope. Some even commit suicide.

Still others approach their lives with the opposite expectation: "If I suffer, I will be worthy of God's Love." Because I was crucified, they think they must be too. These people are casualties of same linear, one dimensional perspective. They think they must be self-effacing to be in God's good graces. When good fortune comes to them, an inner inadequacy undermines their success. Or they experience their good fortune as shameful, squandering their resources or giving them away out of guilt.

Neither self-indulgence nor self-denial bring peace and happiness. Those who indulge themselves eventually see that their substance of choice is addictive and satisfies less and less. And those who deny themselves eventually find that they become brittle, rigid, without sensitivity or compassion.

Most people are either recovering addicts or recovering renunciates. They have experienced the pain of indulgence or the pain of abstinence. Perhaps both. They have made the mistake of acting impulsively without regard for self or others, chasing some satisfaction which always eludes them. Or they have made the mistake of withdrawing from life, avoiding new situations, never taking risks.

Neither extreme honors the person. Both addiction and renunciation are forms of attachment to the past. To stay in the present, each person must learn to accept her experience and all her feelings about it. And this is true for experiences that she dislikes as well as those that she likes. When she is in acceptance of her experience and in touch with her feelings about it, be they negative or positive, she does not have to carry the experience forward subconsciously.

Healing the Divided Self

Both addictive and defensive behaviors are ways of pushing your experience away. They enable you to override the experience, instead of being with it and feeling all the feelings you have about it.

If you could be with all of your feelings and communicate them without being in judgment of yourself, you would not establish a subconscious reservoir of repressed feelings. By detaching from the experience and not feeling the feelings, you create a dual consciousness, part conscious and part subconscious, instead of a singular one.

This type of dissociation happens most obviously in cases of severe physical and/or emotional abuse. Part of the self becomes hidden, inaccessible, split off from the whole. For healing to result, split off aspects of self must eventually be retrieved, along with their traumatic memories, and integrated into conscious awareness.

The reconstitution of the divided self is the essence of the healing process, even for those who have not been severely violated. All fearful experiences cause some form of dissociation, distorting the breathing, and disconnecting the individual from his feelings. These experiences of disconnection from self establish the twisted pathways through which all future victimization occurs.

When parents, teachers and other significant adults do not validate the experience of children, dissociation occurs. Children stuff their feelings and begin to develop a false, socially accepted self which enables them to cope with the demands around them. This self is a sham. It is constructed out of fear, covers over shame, and presents to the world a thin veneer of "normalcy."

All human beings have this false self, this thin veneer,

worn as a mask to protect themselves from perceived judgment and attack. All human beings have the shame of self-betrayal, which they hide from even their closest family members and friends. All human beings have subconscious material that needs to be brought into conscious awareness.

To do this, the thin shell of the false self must crack. The person may lose his job or his primary relationship, or someone close to him may die. Often, he gets a serious physical illness. Once the shell is cracked, the buried material can surface through the cracks.

Since all disconnections from our conscious experience are recorded in the body, all repressed experiences of violation have the potential to manifest as illnesses. As such, illness is a wake up call, a call to awareness and healing. As the psyche of the individual becomes more attuned to love, repressed memories are more likely to come up. That is because the individual is ready to face them, feel the feelings and integrate the experience.

The Resurrected Body

The bridging of conscious and unconscious experience is the primary and essential act of self-integration. All spirituality rests on this integration. The split between body and spirit occurs in the mind. And there it must be healed. The body was never the enemy of spirit. Quite the opposite, in fact. It is the body which cracks the brittle skin of the false self and brings the repressed memories up for healing. Because the body is the cross on which pain is felt, it has a bad reputation. But unless that pain is felt, resurrection is impossible.

Denying the pain of existence does not lift the body up. It does not release pain from the body. Denying the pain is in fact the act of crucifixion. It happens in every moment.

To feel pain is to reunite with the body, to bring breath (spirit) back to the body. In that act of reconnection, the false self is destroyed once and for all. The mask of pretense and denial is broken. Memories return. Experience is integrated.

Pain is not your enemy, but your greatest friend. It brings you back to the body. It brings you back to the breath. It brings you back to the wholeness of your experience.

The resurrected body is a symbol for the re-integration of the split mind. It is the mind in which subconscious has become conscious. It is the mind in which healing and integration are always happening. It is the mind in which forgiveness follows judgment as the outbreath follows the breath in.

Honoring Our Experience: The Dawn of a Surrendered Life

people are forever establishing external standards to measure their spirituality with. These standards are essentially false, because the spiritual life cannot be measured by an outer standard. Even psychological measures like "inner peace" are easily misconstrued, since denial often masquerades as the absence of conflict.

Often, the most difficult and challenging circumstances foster the greatest spiritual growth. Sometimes only the most obvious self-betrayal creates the awareness in which the self will no longer be betrayed.

In the end, we must stop judging our experience and comparing it to that of others. Our experience, with all of its ups and downs, is perfect for us. It brings the lessons we need to learn to move beyond fear and guilt.

To live a surrendered life is to be present moment to moment with our experience. It is to accept our experience without judging it. Or if we judge it, to forgive ourselves for defending, for pushing away. To be with our experience does not mean that we do not space out, detach, disappear emotionally. It means that we become increasingly aware of when we dissociate and gently bring ourselves back.

This "bringing ourselves back" is the essence of meditation. To meditate, it is not necessary to stop thinking.

But it is necessary to become aware of the thoughts as they happen, to see how they take us out of the silence. To see how they prevent us from being wholly present. To meditate is to see how thinking causes us to dissociate, to move away from where we are, to move out of the present moment.

Thinking is not bad. If we make it bad, we will create more thinking about thinking. Thinking is just what happens when the essential self goes to sleep.

Do not make thinking bad. Do not make going to sleep bad or it will be impossible for you to wake up. Waking up for the awakened one is no big deal. It is a totally ordinary experience.

Waking up is what happens when you no longer fall asleep. There is nothing special about it. There is nothing you need to achieve. You are awake right now, and then you forget and go to sleep.

Pain, discomfort, conflict wake you from your sleep. Stop resisting your greatest teachers. Thank them for coming. Thank them for bringing you back to the present moment. They have given you the most profound gift.

In the present, you may just be. You needn't be there for someone else. Being there for someone else is a way of not being present. You needn't even be there for yourself. That too is a trick. Just be. No strings attached. No judgments. No rules. Just be.

That is bliss. That is the flower of acceptance.

Just be. Christ is a being, not a becoming.

New Paradigm Teaching

New paradigm spiritual teachers claim no authority over others. They do not pretend to have the answers for others. They speak only of their own experience. They invite others to share in what they have learned from their experience, and to draw whatever conclusions they will. They do not take responsibility for what others choose to see.

They do not preach. They do not try to fix. They simply accept others as they are and encourage others to find their own truth.

They empower. They see the light in others and encourage it. They don't close their eyes to the darkness, but they know it is ultimately of no significance. When love is present, the darkness dissolves in its light.

They do not deny the darkness or go to battle against it. They know there is nothing wrong, no evil to oppose, no battles to fight. They just gently encourage the light. They know the light itself will heal all wounds.

New paradigm teachers do not try to heal others. They encourage others to heal themselves through self acceptance and self love. They model unconditional love by listening deeply and compassionately, without judging or trying to fix.

The old paradigm teacher wants to heal others and save the world. The new paradigm teacher knows that others are fine the way they are and the world is already redeemed. Why is this? Has the new paradigm teacher closed her eyes? Doesn't she see the suffering in the world, the environmental catastrophe, the endemic violence? Oh yes, she sees the struggle and the pain, but she has a different interpretation of them. She doesn't believe that people are guilty or that the world is doomed. She sees the vast call for love. She sees the universal cry for acceptance and understanding. And that is what she gives.

Not fixing. Not salvation. Not intellectual remedies for physical problems.

Does she give food and medical supplies if they are needed?

Of course, but she remembers to whom she is giving them. She remembers the call and she answers it.

She knows that food is helpful, but it is not the solution to the problem. It is not what is being asked for.

What is asked for is love. Love is the only food. Love is what she gives.

As soon as you see a problem that needs fixing, you have disempowered the person standing before you. Do not do this. Do not accept the pose of powerlessness. There are no victims in the world.

If you see a beggar, don't be taken in. Ask him instead "Why are you standing here begging on this street corner, Oh great one?" Let him know that you see who he really is. Look into his eyes and see his divinity with your own, and then ask him how you can be of help.

You see, powerlessness is a great disguise. Look behind the veil and say "I remember you, brother."

Don't just give the beggar money and walk on without acknowledging him. If you wish to give him money, do so. But do not pass by without acknowledging him. For it is not money he needs, but your love, your blessing, your acknowledgment.

You are not here to fix his life, but to honor him. If you can do this for him, I will do the same for you. For I am not here to fix you, but to call you to yourself. Can you hear? I am speaking to you the same words you said to him: "I remember you, brother. I remember who you are. "

The new paradigm spiritual teacher is content to be a brother or a sister. Content to be the friend. He has met the inner teacher and put all outer authorities aside. And so he does not come to you offering help or asking for it. He comes to you as an equal partner. He treats you as he would like to be treated. And he treats the person next to you the same. There is no pecking order, no preferences.

He does not ask you to follow him. He doesn't trade his knowledge for sexual favors. He does not judge you, isolate you or invalidate your experience. He remains always an equal brother or sister.

When he stands next to you, it is as though you stand next to me. For, in truth, all three of us stand together in that equality. And in that equality is the entire wayward world redeemed.

Equality and Aloneness

Few people are alone with their experience. Most people are afraid to be. The irony is that those who are alone do not feel that they are alone. And those who are not alone, feel lonely.

The lonely seek companionship, yet companionship is not possible, for they have not yet discovered who they are.

The self is a wilderness. Leave it unexplored and cities are built over it.

Explore it courageously and intimacy becomes possible.

True equality requires individuation. Until you know the contours of your own heart you can't learn those of another. If you leave home before you are ready, you look for home without finding it. You find mother instead of wife, father instead of husband.

When you have found your home, you take it with you wherever you go. Find your home first, and then seek companionship.

Find out who you are, not according to someone else's definition, but according to your own. Play with that definition before you accept it. Let all of yourself become present. Explore the dunes that swell up at the sea's edge. Feel the salt spray and walk along the beach at low tide. See all the life-forms, all the possibilities, the play of thought and emotion when the tide is rolled back. Know thyself.

Do not become lost in the world before you know who you are or your chances of waking up are not strong. The world will be only too happy to give you a role and a responsibility. Other people will be only too happy to assign you a role in their play.

Let's face it, some roles are seductive. They promise a lot. It's hard to say no.

"Leave your lonely wilderness and come and live with me. I will love you and take care of you." These are the words the homeless child has been waiting to hear. At last direction has come. The missing parent has materialized. All will be well. Or will it?

Hardly! Rather, this is how the self is betrayed. This is how the wilderness is paved with asphalt, stifling its grasses and trees, invading its sky. Call it domestication, technology, progress. It is anything but that.

The homeless person is always ruthless in making his home. He is without compassion for his environment or for the well being of others. He simply externalizes his anger and his pain.

Try to live with someone before you have learned to live with yourself and you will make a mockery of relationship. It won't work.

Find home inside your heart first.

Only one who knows and accepts himself can find equality with another. Anyone else gives himself away.

It is never the other person's fault when relationship doesn't work. All relationship endings can be attributed to a single cause: lack of fidelity to self.

If you were not faithful to yourself when you entered the relationship, how is it possible that you would be faithful to yourself while you were in it? You see, it can't be the other person's fault. You both just agreed that self-honoring was too rigorous, too lonely. You opted to go to sleep together.

Soon enough you discovered that sleeping together wasn't all it was cracked up to be. You woke up and asked: "Why did I trade one dream for another? The original dream was lonely, but it was also a simpler one.

You just took a detour, a delaying maneuver. You went from sleeping alone to sleeping with another. But the real challenge for you wasn't to sleep, but to wake up. Unless you commit to your own awakening, others can offer you only detours, side-trips, running in place. Time goes by, but nothing changes. The pain doesn't lift. The old dissatisfaction is still there.

In time, you will realize that you have to look at that dissatisfaction. It seems to be a dissatisfaction with the external circumstances in your life, but it remains even after those circumstances have been changed.

The sheets have been changed, but the bed still sags. The problem is not a cosmetic one. It is not a surface one. The problem is in the foundation itself. That is what must be addressed. That is what must be shored up.

Your dissatisfaction says one thing and one thing only: "You are not honoring yourself." If you were honoring yourself, there would be energy and commitment to a vision in your life. You would not be bored. You would not be lonely. You would not be anxious to trade your dream for someone else's.

You are the one, my brother or sister, who opts for the detour. Don't blame the companion who accompanies you. It is not her fault. It is not his fault.

It was simply your choice. Don't beat yourself up over it. Make a different choice. Choose to honor yourself, to step fully into your life.

Make the courageous choice to be alone. Being alone means to be yourself fully. It means to be "all one." It means all the diverse aspects of self have learned to cohere and dance together around a center.

When you fully inhabit your life, you will be drawn to others who are doing the same thing. Then, one person will not have to give up his life for another. Both people can be in their lives and explore how it feels to come together. That is the beginning of a different dance. But it is a dance that cannot happen unless each person is congruent and dancing in his or her own truth.

Moving to a Shared Vision

As the self becomes congruent and learns to manifest its own vision, people come in who share that vision. Yet, notwithstanding the shared sense of purpose, ego struggles will inevitably arise. One person will want a certain configuration or outcome.

Another person will want another outcome. Every relationship will experience the jousting of egos, the beginnings of potential violation or trespass. However, if the sense of self runs deeply enough, neither individual will capitulate to the demands and expectations of the other. There will be a communication of wants and expectations and a willingness to stay open to a solution that honors both sides.

A shared vision is simply that aspect of experience that resonates for both people at the same time. Partnership can be built only on shared vision and the willingness of the partners to let go of their rigid pictures of the way things should be.

Hearing the deep need of each person, but letting go of the ego's pictures of how that need has to be met, the two enter the silence together, asking for the highest good of all concerned. In the silence, each hears something. Sometimes both hear the same thing, or one hears something that the other feels very good about. That is shared guidance. All decisions in a partnership are made through intuitive consensus.

Often the two do not know why they are guided in a particular direction, but they decide to trust it anyway. Great strides are made in this way. Situations that seem etched in stone are transformed. Obstacles dissolve. Possibilities previously discounted present themselves again at the right time. Miracles are experienced.

The surrender of the individual, learned in trusting his own guidance, unfolds into the surrender of the partners, who are learning to trust their intuitive consensus. As couples build skills and confidence in this process of decision making, new groups and communities evolve based on shared vision and directed by shared guidance. You can see the potential this holds for inner and outer peace and harmony.

But one still has to take the first step. One has to honor one's vision and fulfill one's creative purpose. Then one can take the next step and learn how to be fully oneself with another person, surrendering what divides and separates and building on shared purpose.

This is the challenge that lies before you. It is a wonderful and dignified one, one that honors you in every way.

Not Giving Yourself Away

There is a tendency when people go into relationship to "go limp," the way an animal goes limp when it is caught by a predator. There is a kind of "false surrender," a giving away of one's power to the other person. This sets the stage for later violation.

I urge you to go slowly and consciously into relationships so that you do not give yourself away. The desire to please the other, to be liked and accepted, to be loved and adored easily and quickly crosses the line and becomes self-betrayal. You must realize that relationships can be addictive. They can offer you the opportunity to escape from self, to avoid feeling your feelings.

If you are unhappy with your life, a relationship may provide a temporary escape from your troubles, but sooner or later your problems will return. And they will be exacerbated by the demands and expectations of your partner. When your ego agendas emerge, both of you will feel disappointed, if not betrayed. The emotional high of a new relationship promises more than it can ever deliver. If you experience "falling in love," you can be sure that you will experience "falling out of love."

The very expression "falling in love" should tell you that this experience is about self-betrayal. In what other area of life would you allow yourself "to fall" and be whimsical about it? The whole romantic tradition suggests a socially acceptable, nearly institutionalized, form of self-betrayal.

Just as the child creates a false self to cope with the unreasonable demands and expectations placed on him early in life, so does the adult create a "false surrender" to a lover to ease the pain of personal and social isolation. The reason the surrender is false is that it does not withstand the eruption of the dark side. As soon as the unintegrated, unconscious fears arise in the relationship, the feeling of "in loveness" quickly disappears. Were this a true surrender — a sacred union of two people committed to their own and each other's spiritual growth — the dark side would be welcomed into the light of the mutual commitment to truth, authenticity and awareness.

In true surrender, one does not choose the partner just because he or she makes one "feel good." One chooses the partner because, in addition to feeling good together, there is a shared vision and a mutual commitment to growth. There is a context, a healing environment, in which the self is both nurtured and challenged to evolve. This is a conscious partnership. It tends to be at odds with "falling in love," because it is not a giving away of oneself. It is rather a commitment to be present with oneself and the other person through the ups and downs of experience.

Most relationships fall apart as soon as trouble comes along. The promise "to have and to hold, in sickness and in health" is for most people an exercise in absurdity, for many people go to the altar without having taken the time to get to know each other. For this reason, formal marriage should be discouraged until couples have lived together for at least three years. During this time they can discover if they have a mutual commitment to be present for each other.

Most relationships will not survive this three year period of mutual exploration. Indeed, many relationships do not survive the "falling in love" stage. That is because, for most people, relationships are a form of addiction. They are a form of substance abuse, initiated by a mutual desire to "feel good" and avoid the pain, fragmentation and isolation of the self.

Try as they might, no couple can avoid the dark side of experience. Couplehood is never a panacea for the wounds and traumas of the individual psyche. At best, it is an incubation chamber. At worst, it is succession of eruptions, as all our subterranean "faults" are triggered by mutual trespass and violation.

Hard as it is to believe, emotional safety is not to be found in most relationships. That is because most relationships are addictive and temporary. They end in mutual distrust and/or abandonment. Yet when we "fall in love," we have the expectation that they are offering us not only safety, but perpetual bliss. If there ever were a set-up in life, this would have to be it! What better way to punish yourself than to enter into one destructive relationship after another?

The question, of course, is how do we avoid this scenario of "falling in love" and betraying ourselves? The answer is not to refuse to fall in love or to isolate ourselves, but to "fall in love" consciously, or to simply "be" in love.

To be in love is to be present with the other person through all of the ups and downs of experience. To notice the attraction. To notice the judgments that come up. To notice the desire to please or to be taken care of. To see when one feels accepted unconditionally and when one feels conditions have been placed on the gift of acceptance and love.

It means to go into relationship with open eyes, seeing all that unfolds. It means not seeing selectively. Not seeing just what you want to believe.

It means telling the other person the truth about what you feel from the beginning. Not just sharing the mutual admiration and approval, but the fears and the judgments too. It means not hiding the truth from each other.

If you can keep your eyes open as you explore an attraction with someone, you avoid the "false surrender" syndrome. By staying awake through the process, you can avoid the pain and disappointment of waking up a month or a year later and finding out it was just a dream.

It all comes down to one question. "How honest are you willing to be?"

Are you willing to be with your feelings and tell the truth to yourself? Are you willing to be with your feelings and tell the truth to your partner? Do you want to inhabit your life fully or do you want to give yourself away? If you answer honestly, you will know clearly where you stand in your relationships.

As long as you have something to hide, there will be deceit operating in your psyche. Whether it is the deceit of the false self or the deceit of the false surrender matters very little. There is a part of you that is missing in action. Where did it go? And who are you without it?

All masks must be peeled away if we are to stand face to face with ourselves or each other. Until then, this is just a carnival, a public dance ritual the meaning of which has been forgotten.

Remember, brother and sister. I see who you are. I see the face behind the mask. Stop hiding from me. Stop giving yourself away.

Stop chasing pleasure and avoiding pain.

Stand up inside yourself. Be visible. Be vulnerable. Tell the truth. That is what I ask.

Towards Self-Empowerment

I ask you to be rigorous in understanding that no one knows more than you do. No one has anything to give you that you do not already have.

Forget your schools, your teachers, your gurus. Forget your cults of secular and parochial knowledge. Forget your dogmas, your esoterica and your metaphysics. None of this will bring you freedom from suffering and pain. It will only add to the burden you carry.

Be realistic about your experience here. There is only one person who needs to wake up and that is you. Those who have a gift to give you will not withhold it. Those who withhold information or love from you, have no gift to give.

Beware of those who would make you jump through

hoops or stand in line. They are just lining their pockets at your expense. Do not tolerate the idea that salvation lies somewhere else. It doesn't.

Either you hold the key or you don't. If you do, you must begin to use it. If you don't, forget spirituality. If someone else has something you don't, then you and he are doomed together. Better just forget the whole thing and go sailing.

In fact, why not go sailing anyway? Why not do whatever brings you joy? Do you really think you will wake up by doing something serious? I assure you, that is out of the question.

Everything you are serious about will be thoroughly abused until you realize the absurdity of holding anything sacred or apart from life. Enlightenment comes with a great big belly laugh, not a knowledgeable sneer.

Be irreverent in reference to anyone or anything that would prescribe for you or take your freedom away. Don't live by someone else's rules. Live by God's rules. Hold the self in high regard. It is and must remain unassailable. Hold others in high regard. They must always be honored and set free.

But clearly and with good humor let go of relationships with people or organizations who would tell you what to think or what to do. Don't buy the idea that there is something out there to achieve if only you were better behaved, more worthy, more spiritual, more intelligent...you fill in the blank.

Don't line the pockets of those who make empty promises to you. It doesn't matter what they promise: more security, more money, more peace of mind, more enlightenment.

My friend, you are already enlightened. You already have absolute security. You already have peace of mind and all of the resources you need to fulfill your creative purpose. There is only one thing that you do not have. And that is the awareness that all this is true.

And nobody can give you that awareness. Not me, not some used car salesman, not some swami peddling samadhi. If someone tells you he can, it's time for a belly laugh. Put your arm around him and tell him that's the best joke you've heard in fifty years.

Do you hear me? Nobody can give you that awareness! Awareness is not a gift, but a gesture of the self, an energetic movement to be present and embrace life. Awareness exists a priori in all beings.

Simply desire to be aware and awareness is. It comes and goes with the breath. If you want to be aware, breathe! Breathe in to embrace this moment. Breathe out to release it. Breathe, breathe, breathe. Each breath is an act of awareness.

Now if I came to your doorstep and told you I was selling breaths for $5 million a piece, you would think that was pretty funny, would you not? You would tell me, "that's very nice, brother, but I already have all the breaths I need."

Of course you do.

But you keep forgetting that you have them.

You keep buying the insurance policy, falling in love with prince or princess charming, chasing doctor I can make you feel good or swami I've got it all come and get it for five bucks. You know, they all have such long names, it's a wonder you can pronounce them!

Take a breath, my friend. That's right, a deep breath. Nobody has what you need.

Did you hear me? Nobody!

You see, you really are all alone here. But it's not as problematic as you think. Because there is no part of you that's missing. If you just hang around yourself long enough without giving your power away to others, you will retrieve all the fragmented and dissociated aspects of yourself, for no other reason than they never went away. They just got covered over in your race for the exit.

"Just hang around and you'll get it." Great advice from a holy man, right? "I guess we better send this guy to entrepreneurship training or a spirituality and business workshop or he won't make a living."

I have news for you, friends. I don't need to make a living. I AM a living. And so are you.

Just hang around and you'll get it. Because you never lost it. You just pretended to lose it.

One moment you were fully present, and then the next moment your body was there, but your mind was on vacation in the Bahamas. Now, after thirty years or however long it's been, you can bring yourself back, claim your body, and be present in the next moment.

Can you believe that thirty years passed between one breath and another? It may seem strange, but I'm telling you it is a common experience. You needn't be embarrassed.

The next time someone asks how old you are, just tell the truth. "People say I'm forty-five, but I've only taken four breaths!"

I'm just kidding you. Or am I? How many breaths have you taken with complete consciousness, with total presence?

Don't worry about the past. Just begin now. Breathe and claim your life. Breathe and let go of all the mental and emotional crutches you have carried. Breathe and eject all the words ever said to you by every authority figure. Breathe and soften. Breathe and strengthen. Breathe and be. You are authentic. You are intact. You are a child of the great Spirit that animates us all.

Buddha's Window

The Buddha began in the same place where you begin. So did I. The nature of suffering does not change. You have not been given a special handicap, nor were you given fewer abilities. All that apology has to go. There is no difference between you and Buddha, or between Buddha and I.

You are pure being. The Buddha is pure being. You struggle with identification with form. So did the Buddha. So did I.

We are all tested. We all build on quicksand and get sucked down into the muck of conditioned existence. But we are not the conditioned.

All conditions come from us. As soon as we stop placing conditions on our embrace of life, relative existence falls away.

We are the lotus swimming on the murky surface of the pond. We are the awareness, the profound discovery that grows out of the darkness of the conditions. We are the white flower, nurtured by those murky waters.

If you are looking for beauty without sadness, you will not find it. If you are looking for celebration without the poignancy of pain, you will search in vain. All that is transcendent comes from the lowly, the light from the dark, the flower from the mud.

Give up your linear thinking, your rigid, left-brain expectations of what spirituality means. Life is not one dimensional. If you are looking for the absolute, you must find it in the conditional. Indeed, if the absolute is truly absolute, then there is no place where it is not found.

Don't choose one side of the argument. Learn to take both sides and work toward the middle. Both extremes reflect each other. Those who are in conflict share the same lesson.

There is only one way to freedom. Buddha called it the middle way, the way between all extremes.

You can't get there by taking sides. You can't get there by choosing the good over the bad, or the light over the dark. Your path goes through the place where good and evil cross, where the light is obstructed, casting long shadows.

There are no maps that take you to this place. If you ask one person, he says "go to the right." If you ask another, he says "go to the left." If you ask the pessimist where you can find truth, he will say "it was here yesterday. You missed it." If you ask the optimist, he will reply: "it will be here tomorrow."

Who gives the correct answer? Is there, in fact, a correct answer? Or is the expectation of a correct answer itself the illusion?

When you can observe the argument without taking sides, when you can be in the middle of the battleground without attacking anyone, then you have arrived in the place where the lotus blooms. Few will notice you, but it will not matter. You have come home. You have slipped through the veil. You are no longer an object blocking the light, but the window through which it passes.

Can you imagine being a window that lets in the light? That shuts out the cold and opens to let in the fresh air? Can you imagine being so flexible and useful at the same time?

No longer imprisoned in a role, you are glad to be of help. No longer seeking, you are happy to point the way. When someone asks "which way to the divine?" you answer "any way will do."

You know now that the outcome doesn't matter. Only being present on the journey, moment to moment matters. Between now and then, between this and that, the Buddha dwells.

"What a vague, dreamy man," you say. Yes, it is true, his existence spans centuries. Yet, there is no place where he has not been, no heart he has not touched.

If you will allow him, he will touch your heart too. If you will allow him, he will open the window in your mind that separates all sentient beings.

Part 6

Communion
and Community

A Church Without Walls

The community I am calling you to is a church without walls, a place where people of all faiths come together to love, support, and honor each other. My church has nothing to do with what you call Christianity, or with any dogma that separates people. It has nothing to do with any religious hierarchy or elaborate organizational structure.

All are welcome in my church. Both the poor and the rich, the sick and the healthy. Those who call my name and those who call the name of any of my brothers or sisters. I do not stand against any man or woman, but for everyman and woman, for each is God's child. I stand for the sanctity of all beings who in their innocence bless creation with their presence. I celebrate life in all its forms and in its quintessential formlessness.

I urge you to be broadminded. When you enter my church, you do not need to take off your coat or your hat, but please leave your prejudices outside. They have no place in my church. Come to my altar not to hold onto your judgments, but to confess them, to release them to God before your brothers and sisters. You do not have to wear a special hat or robe to enter my sanctuary, but you do have to surround yourself with the awareness of your equality with all beings.

My church is a place of peace and reconciliation. It is a place where fears are acknowledged and trespass is forgiven. My church welcomes all those who admit their mistakes. It casts no one out who seeks the safety of its loving arms.

Many congregations purport to be mine, yet they hold onto their fears and institutionalize their judgments. The stranger and the outcast are not welcome in their sanctuaries. They have built a prison and called it a church. I would rather be worshiped by murderers and thieves than by those who pretend to do my will by judging and excluding others.

Communion and Community

I do not now nor have I ever tolerated hypocrisy. Those who call themselves spiritual guides should set a sincere example for others. They do not have to be perfect, but they should have the courage to admit their mistakes. They should be honest about their humanness. They should step down from their pedestals and learn to empower others.

One should not have lofty, inflated expectations for oneself or for one's spiritual advisors. To ask another person to be mistake free is unrealistic and unkind. Instead, one should ask one's teachers and guides to be honest and direct, to be human. To admit mistakes. To have compassion for the mistakes of others. To create a climate of understanding, safety and love.

That is what my church provides. A safe space. A loving space. A place where each person can connect with his or her spiritual essence.

Undoing Smallmindedness

For thousands of years, people have assumed that they go to church or temple to be with people who believe the same thing they do. If this is true, then churches and temples simply legitimize narrowmindedness and prejudice. Anyone can find someone who agrees with his beliefs. Anyone can create a religion for insiders and exclude those who would challenge his beliefs. This has nothing to do with spirituality. It has more to do with the insecurities of the individual and his tendency to capitulate to the tyranny of the group mind.

Cults thrive on this kind of insecurity. They create a seductive environment that seems to be loving and then proceed to chop away at the ego structure of the individual until he is totally confused, self-doubting and helpless. In the name of spiritual surrender, initiates are asked to capitulate to the authority structure of the cult. In this way, brainwashing poses as enlightenment.

Hierarchical, closed belief systems promise Shangra-la and deliver Alcatraz. They offer freedom from suffering and deliver physical abuse and mind control. Those who are drawn into such situations have lessons around the abuse of power. You can't prevent them from enrolling in this classroom, but you can offer them a helping hand when they are ready to get out.

Fundamentalist groups offer a somewhat less dramatic experience of abuse, but still use the fear tactics of the group mind to control their members. Even traditional churches and temples do not tolerate diversity well. As a result, they lose members who are exploring their spirituality in an authentic way.

Only by honoring the unique spiritual experiences of their membership, while emphasizing areas of commonality, can churches and temples speak to the deeper spiritual needs of their members. Dogma and religious hierarchies no longer make people feel safe and secure. Face to face interactions, simple participatory rituals of singing and dancing that help people open their hearts to each other are what establish the emotional bonds of community. Mutual respect and tolerance for differences are absolutely essential to the creation of a safe, loving space.

It is not necessary for people to have the same beliefs to experience spiritual communion with one another. Communion happens in spite of the mind, not because of it. Communion happens through the extension of love and non-judgment. It can happen anywhere, with any group of people, if they are committed to inclusive, unconditional love.

The time has come for churches and temples to redefine themselves. They must cease to be places where minds cling to linear beliefs in fearful agreement, and become places of self-exploration, where differences are welcome. Love, not agreement, must become the bond that holds the community together.

Communion and Community
Love and the Sword of Truth

Love always challenges you to be flexible about your beliefs and let others into your heart. It always pushes the boundaries of what you are used to (past process) and what you feel is acceptable (group mind agreement). This is a kind of love that you don't easily relate to. Your concept of love is tainted by your ego need for agreement. It is a milktoast version, a soft version of what is the greatest awakening force in the universe.

I offer you the sword I told you I would bring. Use it to remove the the soft, fatty tissues that surround your heart and make your breath labor unnecessarily. Use it to remove co-dependency and victim consciousness from your notion of love. Your version of love is weak, exclusive, hypocritical. It isn't really love at all.

Love has within its essence a great purifying and awakening potential. It offers a kundalini experience that throws off past conditioning. It appears to be gentle and soft, but it is stronger than steel, more powerful than an earthquake.

Love is not only creator but destroyer. It destroys the past. It dissolves what is no longer needed, so that the new may be born. Love is not only the embrace of water that nurtures and sustains, but the fire of spirit that purifies.

John baptized with water and told you I would baptize with fire. When you first hear my words, they are like the crimson flame of dawn gently lifting itself above the horizon's edge. But when my words sink completely into your heart, they will burn like the desert sun or the red-orange flame of the cremation pyre.

I do not offer a milktoast version of love or spirituality. My love for you was not soft 2000 years ago, and it is certainly not soft now.

You see my love as soft, because you are afraid of your anger. You see anger as negative. You do not understand its potential for awakening. You do not realize that anger at injustice is one of the highest forms of love.

When you stop projecting your anger and fear on the world, you can stand for truth without hurting others. You stand not against individuals, but against untruth. Even as you oppose falsehood, you feel compassion for those who cling to false beliefs. You do not criticize them. But you oppose their mistaken ideas with a firmness and clarity that reaches to the roots and exposes the fear and insecurity on which all illusion is based.

When love is broad, it embraces all things as itself. It is like water: feminine, accepting, without discrimination. When love is deep, it destroys all the obstacles in its way. It is like fire: masculine, discriminating, clinging only to truth.

Many of you know the soft, feminine Jesus. But how many of you know the strong, masculine one? The one who brings the sword of discrimination, the sword of truth.

Both are necessary.

If you would know me, you must bring both the feminine and masculine sides together in yourself. Without the masculine side, spirituality is feminine and soft. There is no potential for awakening.

A Living Church

The church I call you to must embrace both the feminine and masculine sides. It must welcome everyone without conditions, yet be devoted to truth without compromise.

In a living church, each person is free to determine her own spiritual path. She is granted total freedom in this pursuit, and in return grants this freedom to others. She agrees not to try to convert or to fix anyone else. She asks for unconditional acceptance and support for her journey and gives the same to others in return.

Anyone who violates this agreement is asked to publicly discuss her motives and behavior and hear the feedback of others. The goal is not to shame or embarrass, but to hear, to be of help, and ultimately to determine whether the individual embraces the spiritual guidelines that govern the community.

All violations of the public trust are dealt with in a loving and compassionate way. The desire is always for understanding and inclusion. But the guidelines must never be watered down or compromised. Spiritual truths should never be adjusted or revised to accommodate people's weaknesses or condone their mistakes.

Mistakes are to be acknowledged and forgiven. To understand what is wrong is to make it right. Such understanding happens spontaneously when individuals are willing to look at their behavior and see how they impact others and themselves. Correction and forgiveness go hand in hand. Without forgiveness, correction is impossible. And without correction, forgiveness is incomplete.

The living church or temple must be clear about and faithful to its process. Since the process is loving, forgiving, and supportive, many different types of people will be drawn in. The flexibility, tolerance and openness of the church/temple and its members will be continually tested. In all this, it must be firm within, and gentle without. All people must be treated fairly and with respect.

In the living church or temple, power always lies in the hands of the congregation. The role of the minister is to lead by example and to empower others to walk their own unique spiritual path. The more successful the minister is in empowering others, the more participatory the organization becomes. Then, it does not matter if the minister leaves, because the programs of the church or temple retain their energy and coherence.

Through empowering others skillfully, a good minister makes himself dispensable. His job is quite simply to help transform old paradigm congregations into new paradigm ones. As a skillful facilitator, he invites others to take responsibility, to share their gifts, and to co-create the organization with him. When the congregation is fully empowered, the minister's work in that place is complete and he will be drawn to a new environment which will challenge him further.

A fully empowered congregation does not need a minister, although it can certainly choose to have one if it wishes. A steering committee made up of both long-time and recent members can guide the church through intuitive consensus, going to the wider congregation to decide important issues. Membership on the committee should rotate so that people do not become attached to their decision-making roles.

Steering committees must take care to remember the example of sharing and empowerment set by the founding minister. They need to help the congregation hold and continue to manifest the original vision of "a safe, loving, non-judgmental space in which people are empowered to share their gifts." If the safety of the space is compromised, or if members do not continue to be actively involved in the church, the new paradigm energy of creative synergy will quickly revert to an old paradigm energy of polarization, separation and struggle for control.

I do not say this to make you into church builders, for frankly the only church you need to attend is the one that lies in your own heart. But if you attend an outer church or temple or wish to attend one, it will be helpful for you to understand the dynamics that can enable you to create a safe, loving space.

All social institutions can be transformed by following the guidelines * I have shared with you. Churches, schools, businesses, nursing homes, prisons, government agencies can all be called to a spiritual purpose through the implementation of these simple ideas.

Three things can be said about my teaching. First, it is

These guidelines are available from the Miracles Community Network, P.O. Box 181, S.Deerfield, MA 01373 simple. Second, it applies to all situations, circumstances and environments. Third, if you practice it, you will find peace in your heart and harmony in your relationships.

You would think these attributes would recommend the teaching, yet look around. Do you see anyone lining up at my doorstep?

Yet cults are springing up everywhere. Fundamentalist religion is booming. People continue to flock in great numbers for darshan with the swamis and gurus.

Don't misunderstand me. I am not against swamis, gurus, fundamentalists or cult members. I'm just pointing out that my teaching — which absolutely works — is not very popular.

Somehow people intuitively understand that if they take up this path, their lives will never be the same. They aren't sure they really want a revolution happening in their lives.

I understand that. Many people like to play at surrender, while retaining their addiction to control. They want to love others who are like them while retaining their judgments about others who are different. That way, they appear to be spiritual, without having to risk becoming vulnerable. They talk about love, but keep a hard shell around them which pushes love away.

They have the semblance of love, but not the real thing. Real love would crack their lives open.

Congruence

Congruence comes through fidelity to self, through the capacity to accept and be with one's own experience, whether or not one's experience is the same or different from the experience of others.

Congruence is exhibited when one's actions are consistent with one's words. A congruent person can be trusted. It's not that he doesn't make mistakes. He certainly does, and he is not afraid to admit his mistakes, to himself or others. A congruent person does not beat himself up when he discovers that he is in error. He finds a way to make amends for his mistake. And if he can't find a way, he forgives himself and endeavors not to make the same mistake again.

A congruent person is always learning from his experiences. He is always becoming more honest with and faithful to himself. And the more honest and faithful he becomes to self, the more honest and faithful he becomes to others. Inner congruence and outer trustworthiness go hand in hand.

The more he knows himself, the more clear he can be with others. He does not make promises or commitments he cannot keep. He says "no" when he means no, and "yes" when he means yes, and "I don't know" when he is not clear. The potential for misunderstanding and abuse is held in check by his willingness to tell the truth about himself.

My teaching encourages congruence as the primary attribute of the awakening process. All loving behavior toward others emanates from inner congruence, which requires that one love, honor and tell the truth to oneself.

As such, the safe, loving, non-judgmental space of spiritual community is dedicated to help the individual come face to face with herself. All her relationships with others, even the most disturbed interactions, will shift when she has learned to tell the truth and honor herself.

My church is a therapeutic community, but without any therapists. Each person is present for her own self-healing and all others are merely witnesses to that. They do not come to analyze her, fix her, or enlighten her. They come simply to accept and bear witness to her process. In trusting her process to lead her exactly where she needs to go, they reinforce their trust in their own process.

My work is always about getting out of the way and trusting the spirit to heal. When we try to become the healer, the minister, the teacher, the technician, we just add more confusion, fear and guilt to everybody's plate. As a result, I do not offer techniques for fixing or salvation. I provide a safe space and offer you the opportunity to stand up and tell the truth about your experience, to yourself and to others. I offer you the challenge of co-creating that safe space and offering to be a gentle witness to others. That is all.

That is enough for a lifetime.

You don't have to have all the answers to grow, to walk through your fears, to inhabit your life more completely. As you tell your story and witness to the stories of others, the alchemical process of transformation begins in your heart. And it, not you or I, is in charge of the journey.

I cannot tell you where that journey will take you. Indeed, it isn't important for you to know. But I can tell you to trust the process and know that it is bringing you home to yourself, home to the most profound intimacy, home to your eternal connection with the divine.

The process is beautiful. It is mysterious. It is beyond prediction, expectation or understanding. Rest in it and all your burdens will be taken from you. Rest in it, and all that is real and true within you will be given wings.

Fellowship

The goal of community is not spiritual instruction, but fellowship. Genuine spiritual community happens only to the extent that it fosters an open mind and an open heart.

You cannot foster an open mind if you teach any dogma. Giving people answers is manipulative and controlling. Instead, help them articulate their questions and begin the search for their answers. Empower them on their journeys of self-understanding. And let them know that the community is a place where they can share ideas without being judged or preached to. Respect the ability of each member to find her way and she will find it.

You cannot foster open-heartedness if you exclude anyone from your community or give preferential treatment to any of the members. People open their hearts when they feel welcome and treated as equals. Nothing closes the heart down quicker than competition for love and attention. Most people are deeply wounded emotionally and react quickly and defensively to even a hint of unfairness, even if it is not intended.

This is why the primary focus of the community must be on clear boundaries and healthy group process. Each person must be given a chance to be heard. Each member must be encouraged not to stuff feelings or hide them from others.

When a safe space is created in which feelings can be expressed without attacking others, misunderstandings, judgments and projections can be dissolved. People can return to their hearts and their bodies. The breath can be restored. Trust can be reestablished.

It is absurd to assume that this kind of physical, emotional and mental reconciliation can happen without a loving environment to foster it. Leaving a group together without teaching them guidelines and process skills is like leaving a toddler alone in a house. He may be okay for the first fifteen minutes, but after that he'll find the chemicals under the sink and the drawer where the knives are stored. You don't want to see the outcome.

And yet you know it. You see it over and over again. As soon as egos rise to attack and defend, it isn't long before the battlefield is strewn with corpses. And then, of course, you have the walking wounded, the ones who have been hit and don't know it yet. You assume that they are normal until you do something to trigger their repressed rage.

No, you don't want to leave a group of wounded people alone to fend for themselves. You want to teach them about boundaries, about how to create and maintain a safe, loving, non-judgmental space. You want to teach them how to communicate their feelings without blaming others or making others responsible for how they feel.

Many people who join spiritual communities are desperate to find love and acceptance. They will say "yes" to the guidelines of the community without understanding them. When the time comes that their buttons are pushed, they may explode in rage, attacking all who get in their way. What do you do in such a case?

Well, you can't read the guidelines to them and ask them to follow them! They aren't going to let you correct them or preach to them. The only thing you can do is to practice the guidelines. Take responsibility for your thoughts and feelings. Don't project. Listen without interrupting. Don't allow yourself to be cut off or steamrolled, but ask that you be heard in the same way that you listened. Do not attack. Do not defend. Just ask for equal time. By not making the other person wrong, but insisting on equality, anger is diffused, and the community receives a living demonstration of the guidelines at work.

A core group of community members must be skillful in practicing the guidelines. Through their ability to model the practice of the process, the entire community learns the process, and then even the most difficult situations can be resolved in a way that honors everyone.

Both the heart and the mind have a tendency to close down. If you don't know this, then you are naive. If you join in community with others expecting everyone to be open all the time, you will have a rude awakening. You will see all these "loving, spiritual" people losing it, acting out their woundedness in unmistakable ways. And you will wonder: "why did I come here? This is just as bad as my nuclear family experience, maybe even worse!"

Well, I will tell you why. You came to get real about the human condition. About your ego experience and that of others. You need to understand that everyone has a dark side. Everyone has unintegrated, traumatic material.

It's time for you to drop your fantasy about what community is. It's not a lovey-dovey experience. It's more like a furnace, fed by the coal everyone is digging up in the other person's backyard. It's neither fun nor pleasant. And, unless process skills are learned early on, it's not very helpful or transformative.

Many people decide to eschew heart-centered, interactive spirituality for this reason. They go off on their separate journeys, meditating six hours a day, pursuing the elongated path of aloneness. But for many of them this is just retreat from the fire. It takes a lot longer to go around the fire than it does to go through it.

But don't attempt to go through the fire without the proper preparation. Don't enter community with others without understanding the depth of the ego's hold on your experience and that of others. Learn how to live with the ego when it comes up. Learn how to be with ego, acknowledge it and let it go. Develop good process skills. Practice the guidelines. Then you can walk on hot coals.

Open Heart, Open Mind

When the mind is closed, the heart shuts down, and vice versa. It doesn't really matter which one closes first, the other one isn't far behind it.

Don't expect the mind to stay open. It won't. An open mind is a mind free of judgments. How long is it before a judgment arises in your mind? Be honest. Is it every two hours, every two minutes, or every two seconds?

In between those judgments, the mind is open. When judgments come up, the mind closes and stays closed for as long as the judgment is held.

Don't try to stop yourself from having judgments. That is a futile exercise. Instead, be aware of the judgments that come up in your mind, look at them, and let them go. If you do this, you will discover that there will be more space between your judgments, more time in which your mind is quiet, relaxed, open.

If you share a safe, loving space with people, use the group presence to acknowledge your judgments. By confessing your judgments to others, you release them even more powerfully than you can by yourself. You also help establish a climate in the community in which ego is acknowledged as a natural phenomena for all people. It comes and it goes. Sometimes with anger. Sometimes with sadness.

You help establish an atmosphere in which no one beats himself up because he is having an ego attack. So the ego is held more lightly, and let go more easily. More humor is brought in. The ego is no longer held by ego, but by something else. Something gentle and allowing. Something merciful, accepting, forgiving.

It doesn't matter what you call it. Some call it Spirit. Some call it Higher Self. Some call it the Presence of Love. Names do not matter.

Whatever you call it, it is the aspect of you that is not anxious or wounded. It is your awareness of the whole in which all the parts rest.

By confessing your judgments, you reestablish your connection to the whole. Open mind and open heart return. By allowing your brother and sister to be your witness, you acknowledge your equality with them. You admit "I too am a person who judges. I am no different than you are."

Through the practice of voluntary confession a community of equals is born. No one is more spiritual than the other. All have judgments. All wish to release them and return to peace.

No one throws stones or criticizes the other because he has a judgment. No one reads him the guidelines. In his acknowledgment of mistake or trespass is your awareness "there go I. I am no different than my brother."

By acknowledging mistakes, there is no pretension to spirituality. There is no desire for perfection, nor shame about imperfection. There is just acceptance of the ego as it rises and falls. There is patience and compassion. This deepens the safety of the space.

When you establish a climate in which the ego is accepted and forgiven, life becomes much easier for everyone. Spirit now holds the ego in its loving embrace and its tendency to split the mind is diminished. As new violations become less frequent and less severe, the wounds of the psyche have time to heal.

This is what my church is all about. A healing community. A community of unconditional blessing and forgiveness. A safe place where ego arises without judgment or condemnation. A sacred space where each contraction, each movement of fear, is gently acknowledged and released. A sanctuary where heart and mind close only to open more fully to the presence of love.

Spiritual Pride

It is spiritual pride to think that you are any further on the journey than anyone else. Even if this were true, it would not serve you to know it or claim it. What serves you is compassion for self, compassion for others. What serves you is knowing that each person has the lesson that is perfect for him and, if he learns it, there is no telling how far he will advance.

Don't think you have the capacity to make a correct determination of the spiritual progress of any individual, including yourself. You don't. You don't know. One who seems to be far behind can move ahead in a flash. And one who seems ahead can be seriously disabled. The whole idea of ahead and behind is meaningless, since you don't know where the starting line is or the finish line.

Others do not necessarily start where you do. They don't necessarily end where you end. Some have a short journey packed with heart-rendering challenges. Others have a long journey composed of many uneventful lessons.

You can look at others and think you understand, but you will just be kidding yourself. You have no idea what anyone else's life is about. Nor is it really any of your business to know.

You have enough on your plate to keep you busy. Just to grasp what your own lessons are and to begin to embrace them is the work of a lifetime.

If you are a spiritual teacher, ask yourself if you have chosen that role to avoid learning the lessons you came here to learn. By being an authority and prescribing for others, you never have to look at yourself.

Rest assured, you won't be able to hide forever. In time, your own dirty laundry will be aired. It is inevitable. Everybody comes here and thinks he can do a disappearing act. Some people are real good at it. They disappear for fifty or sixty years. When they come back they are sure no one will recognize them. But as soon as they walk into the grocery store, they know the game is up.

Nobody can hide forever. Because this is a place where everybody gets found. Everybody gets the wake-up call, eventually. That's the nature of the physical journey. You might as well get used to it.

Even those of you lingering at the end of the line will eventually get your turn. The man calling out names is not going to die before he gets to you. And even if he did, someone else would replace him. You can't hide here. You can't become permanently invisible.

Perhaps that seems odd to you. After all, the majority of people on planet earth are either wearing clever disguises or pretending not to be home when the doorbell rings. That is how pervasive the denial is.

But it doesn't matter. These people are not running the show. The one behind the mask is making all the decisions. The one behind the mask calls the stranger to the doorstep to deliver the wake up call.

We think the authority is outside and it's all just happening to us. Not so! The authority is inside and we are all making it happen so that we can wake up.

The entire planet is on a wake-up mission. That is why so many people appear to be asleep. How could they wake up unless they were sleeping or at least pretending to be asleep.

This is not the planet to be on if you want to hide. It is not the place to be if you want to stay asleep. If your goal is unconsciousness, you are in a dangerous place!

All the people who are now sleepwalking will one day realize that they have left their beds and houses and are walking in the street. They will do that quite simply: by bumping into each other.

That is what the interactive journey is all about: trespass, collision, abuse, call it what you will. It seems to be intentional, but it really isn't. Nobody consciously knows he's going to bump into someone else. It just happens. And then, if he's smart, he wakes up and says "Oh, sorry, I didn't see you." And his sister says "No problem. I didn't see you either."

What else is she going to say? If she takes it personally and says "Yes, you did see me you jerk!" what will that prove? It doesn't prove that she was attacked. It just proves that she feels attacked.

And that's what you really have out there: a bunch of people who feel attacked. It's not an accurate picture of what's happening, but it is the one that is popularly accepted. That is because everybody interprets behavior. Everyone assigns intention. Everybody thinks he knows the other person's motive. But, of course, he doesn't. He doesn't have any idea why someone bumped into him.

You've heard of arranged marriages? Well, this was an arranged bumping. Both people behind the masks decided to deliver a reminder to each other so that they could both wake up at the same time. When they arranged the meeting, they had no idea that they would both feel attacked when it happened.

That's because in arranging the meeting, they were in touch with each other's intention: to honor, to assist, not to harm or to hurt. Because they trusted the other's intention, they weren't concerned about what happened specifically. They knew, whatever it was, it would be okay.

If you were in touch with everybody's intention to wake up and help you wake up, you could not take any trespass personally. You would just say "Sorry, brother. I didn't see you. Thanks for the wake up call. I'll be more alert now."

It's not the bumping that wounds, but the interpretation of the bumping. The condemnation of the bumper. The condemnation of self for being bumped. As soon as we call it abuse, we lose sight of our role in it. We project the responsibility onto someone else. We think we were just sitting there minding our own business and along came this nasty person who attacked us.

That's not what happened. That's the big self-deception, the big lie we try to pass onto others. We try to talk to each other as victims and wonder why everyone keeps getting beat up.

There is no meeting without honesty and personal responsibility. There is no meeting without self forgiveness and compassion for others.

If we want to meet, if we want to wake up together, we must stop interpreting what happens and just let it be. We can be startled by the bump. We can tell the other person we are surprised. But let's not think we understand why it happened. Instead, let's ask. Let's check it out.

Let's communicate honestly and unpretentiously: "When we bumped into each other, it was painful for me, brother? How was it for you?" Telling the truth by taking responsibility for our own feelings is not an attack or presumption of trespass or guilt. It is just a simple sharing of experience. It invites dialogue, not separation.

Once guilt is presumed, attack is inevitable. You cannot attack an innocent person. To attack you must believe your attack is justified, that the person deserves it. At this point, you have dissociated from your own feelings, split your mind in two, and prepared for the inevitable outward skirmish. All because of spiritual pride, all because you thought you knew the other's motive.

Give it up, my friend. You don't know what is in your brother's heart. You will never know. The best you can do is ask him openly. This is as close as you will ever come to knowing what he thinks and what he feels.

If you never inquire of your sister what her experience

is, how will you ever come to know her? All you will know are your own projections, your own judgments and interpretations. These say a lot about you and very little about her.

And, if you cannot presume her innocence, how will you ever be able to presume your own? If you think you know her, how much better must you know yourself?

You see, there is no way out. Every judgment you make about someone else returns to haunt you.

Better to give those judgments up. Better to realize that you know nothing of other people's intentions or motives. Better to understand that you are often completely out of touch with your own intentions.

Spiritual pride contributes only to your continued ignorance. An arrogant person does not grow. She does not become transparent to herself or others. She hides. She attacks covertly and when confronted appears to be asleep. She plays cat and mouse with herself and the universe.

I will give you a better game to play. It's called: "I'll bump you if you bump me." No blame, no shame. You don't even have to keep score. Just bump away until you wake up and look into each other's eyes without condemnation or judgment.

Part 7

Opening
to Miracles

The Miracle of Self

The greatest miracle you will ever experience does not lie outside of you. It lies within. That miracle is your very existence. That you exist at all is a testimony to God's love.

When you are in touch with God's love for you, everything that happens in your life is miraculous. All you see are extraordinary opportunities to love, learn, create and be fully present in your life.

When you are not in touch with God's love for you, everything that happens in your life seems not to be good enough. You perpetually find fault with yourself, with others and with your experience.

Your relationship to yourself and your creator determines the quality of your life. When you feel worthy of God's love, you talk to God, confide in Her and are grateful for your life. When you feel that you are just a random, purposeless creation, you have no one to talk to. You lead an isolated, aimless life. You do not know why you are here.

Purpose in life comes from the connection to the divine. It comes from the self-affirmation "I matter. There is something here I am meant to do. God has a plan for me."

Miracle consciousness depends on our ability to feel or intuit the presence of God in our life. And the ability to intuit God's presence depends on our willingness to trust ourselves, to trust others and to trust our life as it unfolds.

Learning to Trust

To learn to trust you must experiment being neutral about what happens in your life. You don't have to see things in a positive light. Just stop seeing them in a negative light. Stop imposing your expectations on the events and circumstances of your life. Just let life unfold and see what happens.

God doesn't ask you to convert yourself. She doesn't ask you to chop off your intellect and believe on faith. She makes a far more simple request. Just stop judging, stop finding fault, stop imposing your expectations, your will, your interpretation, your pictures of reality, and see what happens.

She says a very simple thing to you. She says: "You think you know what's going on, but you are not happy. Your knowledge, your judgments, your interpretations are not bringing you peace or fulfillment. So set them aside for a few moments. Give life a chance. Experience it free of the limitation you place upon it."

When you do this, you get incredible results. Things go smoother. Problems resolve. Relationships move on course. Your life starts to work. All because you gave up the idea that you "know" what your life is for.

You see, if you are going to let God be in charge of your life, you have to give up the idea that you "know." Increasingly, you develop the attitude that your job is just to show up, to be present, to let things happen. You know you are not the one who makes your life work. So you stop trying. You stop trying to figure things out. And you just show up and do what you are asked to do in the moment.

You can't know God's plan as long as you insist on your own. God can't be in charge as long as you think you are the boss.

The first block to your relationship with God is your knowledge and your pride. Surrender these and you will make room for God's plan in your life. Giving up your agenda is the same thing as opening to Hers.

What is God's agenda? It is healing, reconciliation, joyful self-expression and intimate communion. God's agenda is to make miracles everywhere. Wherever your ego sees a problem or a limit, God's Will is to birth a miracle.

Your ego's tendency is to keep things as they are, no matter how bad they may be. God says: "let go of the past and make room for something that honors you more deeply." You are afraid to do that because there is no guarantee that the new will be any better than the old. You'd rather hold onto the old and invite the new in at the same time. That is the inevitable Catch 22. The new cannot come in until the old is released. When you are attached to the past, you cannot move toward the future. And your experience of the present is one of deadlock.

Letting go of the past is never easy. Yet it is the only act that brings the presence of God into your life. When you let go of what used to be and accept what is, the universe instantly moves to support you. The deeper your let-go is, the more resources rush to your side.

It is the nature of the ego to become attached to the past. It is the nature of the ego to project the past forward into the future, to meet the new with conceptual nets that would tame it and make it conform to yesterday's experience. There is nothing new in this. It is simply the movement of fear which resists anything new.

It is important to see how that fear operates in your life. It is important to realize how you become attached to your previous experience and resist anything new that wants to come into your life.

When you hold onto your experience or use it to interpret the present experience, you "take control" of your life, and push God away. When you surrender your ideas about the way things should be, let go of the past, and open to the future, you invite God back into your life.

Your ego will not do this without a struggle. Its job is to keep you safe. And, if it fears for your safety, it will push even God aside. You need to make a deal with your ego. You need to do an experiment. You need to say to your ego "I know you are scared, but I'd like to let go this one time, and see what happens."

When the ego sees that it won't be threatened by inviting God in, when it realizes that you can take risks and be safe too, it will stop fighting you so hard. Every time you let go and trust and have a positive experience, the ego will take note.

Unfortunately, it will still argue that you should do it the way you did it last time. It will still argue for the past, for what is familiar, because it is basically uncomfortable with change. Its job is to create continuity and change seems to threaten that.

But what is continuity but a projection of the old upon the new? If something is continuous, it is not miraculous. Miraculous events are not continuous with what happened before them. They represent a shift of energy. A movement out of past perception, past limitation. They are unpredictable, unexpected, and in many cases inscrutable.

We call them miracles because God's hand is in them. But without our permission, they could not take place. Without our surrender of the past, miracles could not come into our lives. We prepare the ground for them. We create the space in which the miraculous occurs.

Miracles and the Unmiraculous

There is a great deal of confusion regarding what a miracle is. Some people are cured of serious illnesses, are delivered unexpectedly from dangerous situations or experience unanticipated good fortune. All of these situations are indeed miraculous. But what about the person who dies of an incurable illness, who is paralyzed in a serious accident, or is the victim of some terrible crime? Are we to view these apparently negative events as completely unmiraculous, as out of sync with God's laws? And, if so, can we say that those who experienced these negative events were people who were not spiritual or close to God?

Nothing could be further from the truth. All events cohere in a higher order, the meaning of which dawns on those who open their hearts and minds to their experience. No event, no matter how unfortunate, is devoid of purpose.

The cripple is no less holy than the man whose broken

limbs are mysteriously healed. Don't make the mistake of thinking that you can have miracles on demand. Don't be foolish enough to believe that if you don't get the miracle you want, you must not be holy.

Linear thinking is always dangerous, but when applied to issues of spirituality, it becomes almost deadly. You are not bad if you don't receive the miracle you ask for. You are not good if you do. Such thinking comes from looking only at the surface of life. And, if you want to understand the miraculous nature of life, you must look beneath the surface.

All events are miraculous in the sense that they have a higher purpose. They belong to God's plan. Often, we don't see what that purpose is and we feel betrayed by God. We think we are being punished. But that is just a limitation on our part, an unwillingness to accept, to trust, to look more deeply for the meaning that now eludes us.

The real miracle does not lie in the outer event, in the apparent good or bad fortune involved. The real miracle lies in the spiritual purpose behind the event. The purpose may be to strengthen our faith or to challenge it. It may be to strengthen our body so that we can better serve, or to weaken our body so that we can leave its limits behind.

We are not capable of deciding what anything means. All we can do is ask: "What is this for? What is the meaning of this?"

Miracles help us break through the limits of our own mind. They challenge our world view. They urge us to let go of our interpretation of life so that we can see the possibilities that lie beyond it.

It is odd, perhaps, but sometimes an apparent tragedy turns out to be an unanticipated blessing. You have heard people say "Thank God for my Cancer. Without it, I never would have transformed my life." Or "Thank God for the lesson of my child's death. It helped me wake up to my purpose in this lifetime."

Sometimes what appears to be taken away is the

greatest gift, because it calls us forward. It brings us out of our shell into our life purpose.

If we really want to open to miracles, we must stop telling God what a miracle is. We must stop giving God instructions on how to take care of us.

We must realize that God knows what is going on. We don't know how She knows, but it doesn't matter. The more deeply we look, the more signs we receive that Her work is wisdom and compassion in action.

Miracles and Physical Laws

Since the real Miracle is our joining with God by understanding His Will for us, external healing is not required. It may happen or it may not. We may be cured of our illness or we may not. The real miracle comes in our surrender to life as it is. When we come to peace and acceptance of our life, the miracle of God's love dawns in our heart.

Some people feel that a miracle has not taken place unless a physical law is transcended. The ocean parts and lets the people pass, the bars of the prison dissolve in thin air, the corpse is raised from the dead.

I hate to disappoint you, but these things don't happen. Everything that happens on the physical plane happens according to physical laws. That is the nature of the experience here.

That does not mean that spiritual laws are not in operation. They certainly are. But spiritual laws work with and through physical laws. There is no contradiction.

Spiritual law has nothing to do with how things work, but with the interpretation of your experience. It is the decision you make about what an event in your life means. And that decision determines your psychological experience of the event.

For example, I was crucified. Had I had superhuman

physical powers, I could have stopped the crucifixion from happening. But my spiritual understanding did not make me a superman. It simply enabled me to see the truth of what was happening to me. So I did not take the crucifixion as an attack. I did not condemn my brothers, for I saw that their actions were motivated by fear. And I felt compassion for them.

Yes, I was crucified. But I did not close my heart. I did not cast blame on anyone. I surrendered to God's will in that moment, as I had done in every other moment of my life.

If you think your faith will stop the crucifixion, you are just as likely to be wrong as right. Perhaps your faith will help your executioners open their hearts and change their minds. Perhaps it will not. Perhaps your faith will simply allow you to suffer your fate without condemning others.

You see, you don't know what God is asking from you until He asks it. And then, your choice is either to resist or surrender.

It is that way in any moment of your life. It is that way in any situation. You don't know what it means. You just need to come to it willing to let go, willing to allow, willing to surrender.

Those physical laws which appear to be vitiated in certain miraculous experiences are simply laws that are incompletely understood. If you understood the laws fully, you would see that the event occurred entirely in harmony with them.

Of course there is much that you do not understand about the laws that govern physical reality. As your understanding of physical reality matures, you will increasingly see how physical laws interact with spiritual laws to create the experience you need in each moment.

Visualization is powerful. Any exercise which alters perception can assist in healing, but that healing will take place according to physical laws. I strongly discourage magical thinking, or the attempt to alter physical reality through the concentration of the mind. It is not that such things are impossible, but they are improbable and represent an aspect of your experience which does not need to be tampered with. To stand in the middle of the train tracks with the train approaching, while visualizing the train disappearing, is not something I recommend.

Miracle mindedness is not demonstrated through the attempt to manipulate physical reality with the mind. That is an activity of the ego. The attempt to produce miracles on demand is the activity of a clown, not a spiritual man or woman.

You demonstrate your miracle-mindedness by surrendering to your experience and connecting with God's will for you in each moment. Your job is not to try to alter physical reality but to be fully present with it. As you endeavor to do this, your fear, your addictions, your attachment to the past, will rise up before you. Your job is to meet that fear, those addictions and attachments in a loving and compassionate way. Your job is to make a safe space for you to feel your feelings, to walk through your fear and your pain. Your job is to drop all your interpretations, concepts, judgments and enter the experience open and undefended. Your job is to meet the wounded child with love and encouragement. To invite him to step forward. To tell him that it's okay to be afraid, that there is nothing here that will hurt him, because you are present with him. That is how healing happens and the miracle of self unfolds.

Everything Can Be Lifted Up

Every experience you have can be lifted up through the power of your unconditional acceptance and love. Every experience, no matter how seemingly painful!

God does not work alone. He needs your cooperation. You should not work alone either. When you try to live depending on yourself alone, you stumble and fall. Only when you think and act beyond your immediate ego needs does your life become subject to the law of grace.

To honor and care for yourself is your responsibility. Anything that honors you cannot possibly hurt another. But to act in a selfish way, placing your good above another's, invites conflict and resentment. The ways of the world are harsh in this regard. One who takes advantage of others may be feared but he is not loved. When his fortune changes, which it invariably does, and he begins to self-destruct, others are more than happy to help pull him down.

The outside world inevitably reflects back to you the fruits of your thoughts and actions. That is why we say "As you sow, so shall you reap."

When you act without regard for others, you do not honor yourself. Every time you attack, you have something to defend. You are always looking over your shoulder to see who or what might be sneaking up on you. This is not a particularly satisfying or dignified way to live. Your fearful thoughts and actions call forth the fearful thoughts and actions of others.

These fear-based interactions become institutionalized in your "eye for an eye" system of justice, which perpetuates the cycle of abuse. By making the perpetrator into a victim, you hope to discourage him from brutalizing others in the future. You don't understand that all of his rage comes from his perception of himself as a victim and it is that which you are reinforcing by punishing him.

If you want to change the criminal, you must stop punishing him and begin to love him. Nothing else will work.

Love is not a reward for his trespass. It is the redeemer of his soul. It recalls him to himself. It shifts him out of the reactive cycle in which he dehumanizes himself and others. In the face of genuine love and caring, even the most vicious criminal softens.

You cannot stop hate by fighting it with revenge. Every act of violence begets a counteract. By now you should know this.

It would be so easy if all you needed to do to contain violence was to meet it with force. That would be a religion and world view you could easily understand. But were this the case, there would be no hope of spiritual awakening on the planet. So it cannot be the case. The "eye for an eye" system of justice is not built into the blueprint for healing on planet earth. The only thing which can bring freedom from violence is that which is itself free of violence.

Only a spiritual solution works. Human solutions to human problems invariably fall short. You can't solve a problem on the level on which you perceive it. You must go to a higher level, see the big picture, see the cause of the problem and address that.

That is why you need God in your life. That is why you need a spiritual practice. That is why you need something that calls you out of the cycle of attack and defense in your life.

There is no peace without God.

You can't find peace in the world. You can find it only in your heart, when it is open.

An open heart invites the beloved in. It invites the stranger in, and yes, even the criminal. An open heart is a sanctuary where all are welcome. It is a temple where the laws of spirit are practiced and celebrated. It is the church you must enter again and again to find redemption.

Ask yourself "Am I thinking and acting for myself alone, or do I have the good of the other in my heart?" If you do have his good in your heart, you will lift him up and you will be lifted up with him. If you don't, you will retreat in fear, closing your heart, seeking more protection.

It is a simple choice. Crucifixion happens when your heart closes to your brother. Resurrection happens when you open your heart to him, when you stop blaming him for your problems, when you stop punishing him for his mistakes, when you learn to love him as you love yourself. Only this will bring release from the prison of fear. Only this!

Love is the only miracle. All other "miracles" are frosting on the cake. Look beneath the surface of every one of them and you will see a shift from fear to love, from self-protection to self-expansion, from judgment of others to acceptance of them.

Love says: "I accept you as you are. I will consider your good equally with my own." Do you have any idea how powerful this statement is? To every person you address in this way, you offer freedom from suffering. And by offering it to him, you offer it to yourself.

If you do not seek equality, then you will never learn how to give love without conditions. It you do not offer equality, you will never learn how to receive unconditional love.

What you seek, you will find, As you offer, so shall you receive. The law has not changed.

A Wolf in Sheep's Clothing

For some, it is a great challenge to consider the well being of others. For others, it is far too easy. In fact, it is easier for them to meet the needs of others than it is for them to get in touch with their own needs. In this case, serving others can be a form of self-betrayal.

When one opens his heart, he includes others in his sense of well-being. He does not trade their well-being for his own. He doesn't try to please others at his own expense. He does not give himself away and find an identity in someone else.

He expands his territory of caring to include his family, his friends, and ultimately his enemies. He expands his sense of self continually, as he learns to open his heart and soften to his experience.

In this way, his love extends outward. It starts in his embrace of himself and his own experience. It starts with his fidelity to self. And then it reaches out to embrace other people he cares about. He respects and cares for their experience too. He encourages them to honor themselves. He has their highest good at heart.

By contrast, one who tries to please others at the expense of self is not offering love, but sacrifice. And sacrifice has its price. Hidden in the apparent show of selflessness is the demand for recognition, the desperate search for approval, the need to insure acceptance and love at any price.

Because hidden demands eventually surface, the one who is the recipient of the sacrifice usually feels manipulated and controlled. There is the sense that one is beholden to the other person. One stays in the relationship not out of joy in the other's presence, but because of guilt. "How can I leave her? Look at what she's done for me. And, if I did leave, she would not make it. She'd self-destruct. She'd commit suicide!"

Ironically, the very people who have been cared for "so selflessly" themselves become custodians and caretakers. Roles reverse. The sacrificers extract their side of the bargain. Or if they can't, there is great bitterness on their part, which feeds the guilt of the recipients.

Beware of those who would sacrifice their lives for you. They will insist that they are repaid for every self-effacing gesture. Anyone who offers to give himself away for you will expect you to do the same for him.

You have heard the expression "there is no free lunch." That is ultimately true. But there are lunches that appear to be free. You don't have to pay now, but you most definitely have to pay later. Generally speaking, you can assume that what you don't have to pay for now is given on credit. Eventually the bill collector will come and he will want interest too!

Better not to accept the deal when it is offered to you. Better to say: "No, sister. I would prefer that you honor yourself. Please do not ignore your needs because you wish to please me. Nothing good can come of it. " I realize this is not the popular thing to say. It wasn't a popular thing for me to say two thousand years ago either!

The devil's invitation comes in many guises. But his favorite one is some version of the free lunch. Watch out when food, money, sex or attention is offered to you "without strings attached." The longest strings are the ones that are invisible!

If you are responsible, if you have the ability to pay, a free lunch does not appeal to you. If you can go into an elegant restaurant, order a good bottle of Cabernet Savignon, and eat Filet Mignon and Baked Shrimp on the deck overlooking the water, why would you go to the local soup kitchen?

You would do it only if you were greedy. Only out of greed would you make yourself or others you care for "sacrifice" their well-being today in order to reap imagined riches in the future. I have news for you: that future never comes! It is undermined by your behavior right now. Greed does not bring a kind or happy future, nor does a miser enjoy his wealth. Death comes too soon for those who do not seize the moment and live it fully.

If you are a responsible person, you pay your way up front. You support others by purchasing their services. You know that receiving without giving is out of harmony with nature and the divine will. You don't seek that which is unfair, no matter how seductive it may appear.

Fairness

To be a fair person is to demonstrate miracle mindedness. To give what you have and take what you need keeps the flow of resources moving. To give less than you have or take more than you need creates an imbalance in the flow of resources. To try to give more than you have or to take less than you need also creates imbalance.

No one but you can determine what you have and what you need. That is why no system of economics, no matter how pure, can create a fair distribution of the collective resources of human beings. Only fair people can create a fair economy.

Fairness happens voluntarily. It never happens by control. People have to be free to make mistakes and learn from them. Otherwise, the system is not open and growth is not possible.

Fairness is learned through the experience of inequality. People who take more than they need or give less than they have usually feel they have been treated unfairly in the past. To establish balance, personally and financially, they need to work on their anger and resentment.

By contrast, people who take less than they need or try to give more than they have usually feel guilty for treating others unfairly in the past. To establish balance, they need to work on their guilt.

When the victim resolves his anger and resentment, he no longer needs to take more than he needs. Then, he does not have to become a victimizer to equal the score.

When the victimizer resolves his guilt, he no longer needs to give away the resources he needs. Then, he does not have to become a victim to create balance.

Once you understand your pattern and see how your life has gone out of balance, you can begin to correct it. If you are a giver, you can learn to be a receiver. If you are a receiver, you can learn to be a giver.

When giving and receiving become equal in your life, fairness will be established in all of your relationships. By demonstrating fairness, you will be witnessing to the miracle of equality. You will no longer tolerate deception in yourself or in others. You will stand for justice wherever you go. You will demand that each person be given the love and respect which is his due.

Part 8

Reconciliation

The Great Equalizer

If you look at the surface of people's lives, you would have to say that people aren't equal. One person is a great athlete making millions of dollars a year. Another person is a handicapped veteran living on disability. One person has several advanced degrees. Another has not even finished the eighth grade. This hardly seems equal or fair. Indeed, in the eyes of the world, there is very little equality.

Yet, in the eyes of Spirit, people are completely equal. The rich man has no more privilege than the poor man. The simple man is no less appreciated than the brilliant intellectual. When you see beyond appearances, when you see what is in people's hearts, you see the same struggle, the same pain. The wealthy doctor who has lost a son to AIDS has the same pain that the woman on welfare has when she loses her daughter.

Pain is the great equalizer. It brings us all to our knees. It makes us more humble and sensitive to the needs of others. Pain is the greatest teacher on planet earth. It undermines all hierarchies. It dissolves social status and invalidates material riches. It brings everything up for healing.

If you have touched your own pain deeply, you know this. And you feel great compassion when you see others in pain. You do not need to push them away, nor do you need to try to fix them. You just hold them deeply in your heart. You offer them a hug and some words of encouragement. You know what they are going through.

The world builds people up and it takes people down. There is no permanence in the world. Fame and ignominy, poverty and riches, happiness and despair run hand in hand. You can't experience one side without experiencing the other. If you think you can, you are in denial.

Most of you are in some degree of denial. That is probably because you have hardly touched your pain. It is too scary to do so. You would rather pretend to be spiritual than admit that you are having a really rough time. You don't want people to see your dirty laundry: your judgments, your yearnings, your suicidal thoughts. It is easier for you to let people see the pasteboard mask than the contorted face behind it. You are proud of the spiritual adult, but you are still ashamed of the wounded child.

The worst thing about denial is that it creates a culture of pretense and shame. Because so many people are pretending to be well-adjusted spiritual beings, those who are in touch with their pain feel that they are social misfits. They feel that they are not worthy to associate with such bright beings. They feel ashamed of their pain. And so they isolate themselves from others or they are rejected by others who feel threatened by their emotional honesty.

One who is in touch with her pain immediately cuts through all the pretense in human interaction. Her willingness to be emotionally present with what she is feeling tends to bring up feelings in others that they may not want to deal with.

Yet for those who have the courage to be with their pain, a sacred passageway opens. The closed heart stretches and opens, the body begins to breathe, and blocked energy is released. This is the first step in the healing process. In the acknowledgement of pain and the willingness to be with it, the sacred journey begins.

One cannot find genuine intimacy with others without being deeply with one's experience and communicating honestly about it to others. Relationships based on mutual denial are emotional prisons. Since two masks cannot communicate, partners in such relationships have no tools to open the prison door.

Enter an awakening crisis — the death of a loved one, a physical illness, or the loss of a job — and presto, the shell of denial is cracked. The prison door is blown open and the shell shocked inhabitants are led out into the fresh air. Here they feel worse than they did when they were in prison, because now they are in touch with their pain.

Awakening events take chronic pain and make it acute. It hurts more. We get sicker. We can't function in the world as well. We have to make time and space to be with our situation. Since we weren't ready to choose this consciously, we had to do it unconsciously. It seems that we got a curve ball from God, but really it was just the universe responding to our weak, muted cry for help.

To begin to "feel" our pain is the first great act of self-liberation. It is the end of unconscious sabotage and collusion. It is the birth of conscious awareness.

When we "feel" our pain we begin to move through it. It is a passageway, a means of shifting our lives. It is not meant to arrest us. We are not meant to fall in love with our pain, hold onto it, or build a new identity around it. It is not a stationary train, but a moving one. Once we get on it, it takes us where we need to go.

Pain is the great equalizer. It enables us to be honest and authentic. It empowers us to ask for unconditional love and support from others and to be willing to offer the same in return. It connects us with a healing community. We meet other human beings whose shells of denial are cracking. And we begin to heal together.

The decision to heal is often a lonely one, yet no one ultimately needs to heal alone. Our healing is much quicker and much more profound when we are witnesses to the healing of others.

A healing community is very different from a hospital, where people go to get fixed or die isolated and alone. In a healing community, people are connecting with their feelings and discovering greater intimacy with others. In a healing community, people may die, but they do not die alone. They die surrounded by loved ones. They die having stepped more fully into their lives. They die in forgiveness, in acceptance, and in peace.

It is time to stop building hospitals and start creating healing communities. Don't do this for other people. Do it for yourself, for your family, for your friends. You all need a safe, loving space in which to heal.

When pain is faced, people meet as equals. When pain is acknowledged, people learn to tell the truth about their experience. Then God's work can begin on planet earth.

Addiction to Pain

Just as dysfunctional as the denial of pain is the addiction to pain as a way of life. Some people who begin to acknowledge their pain see that it gets them lots of attention. They build a whole identity around being wounded, being a victim of their experience. They become addicted to telling their war stories.

When someone tells the same story over and over again, you know that person is not being authentic. The authentic person is not a professional storyteller. He is not a confession artist. He does not need to be the center of attention to feel good about himself.

The authentic person tells his story because the telling of it is an act of healing. As he tells it, he comes to a more profound insight into and acceptance of what happened. He embraces his experience more fully. He deepens his compassion for himself and others. As he tells his story, he heals, and so others heal with him.

The moment he has integrated his experience, he no longer needs to tell his story. If he insists on telling it, it becomes an impediment to his spiritual growth. It becomes a crutch that he leans on, even though his limbs have healed and he is ready to put all his weight on them. He becomes attached to his story, wedded to his pain. He becomes a fraud and an imposter. His story is an act. It no longer empowers people.

The acceptance of pain brings a shift away from dis-ease. It brings increased ease, self-acceptance and confidence. It allows one to take the next step on one's journey.

Acknowledged pain is a door that opens, an invitation

to expand, to trust more and take more risks. As we step into our fear and our pain, we move toward our joy. We leave old limits in our lives behind. We shed our old skin.

As we share authentically, we empower ourselves and others. We move on. They move on. A life of pain is no longer called for. In fact, it is unnecessary.

Pain is only necessary where there is dissociation or denial. Suffering happens only when we are in resistance to our life. While pain and suffering are universal phenomena, they are temporary ones. They touch every life at one time or another. But they are not constant companions. They are messengers, not roommates.

To say that the messenger is not present in our lives when he is standing at our door is utter foolishness. Let us answer the door and hear what he has to say. But when the message has been heard, the messenger can leave. His job is over.

Therapeutic Abuse

When the work of healing becomes pop art, a culture of unhealed healers is born. When it becomes "chic" to be a victim of childhood trauma or sexual abuse, therapists too easily get away with putting words in their clients mouths. Memories of events that never happened are enshrined on the altar. Incidents of minor insensitivity or carelessness are exaggerated and painted with the language of guilt. Everyone imagines that the worst must have happened. This is hysteria, not healing. It is a new form of abuse.

Instead of inquiring into what happened and allowing the inner wounded one to speak, a professional label is placed on the wound. Instead of empowering the victim to find his voice and connect with his experience, his voice is squelched once again. And he is given someone else's opinion of what happened to him. In order to gain approval, the wounded child tells the story the authority figure — his therapist — asks him to tell. By capitulating to authority, he is told he is getting well.

The therapist projects her own unhealed wounds onto her client. Her subjectivity is taken for objectivity by the courts. Families are separated. More children are punished. The chain of abuse continues.

The attachment to pain is debilitating. The embellishment, exaggeration or fabrication of pain is insane.

Just as the creation of a priestly class of authority figures undermined the organic spirituality of the church, so the creation of a new class of therapist/healer authority figures undermines the ability of individuals to access the healing that is their birthright.

You can't make anyone heal any more than you can make people act in a moral way. Healing is a voluntary act. It happens as people are ready. Many people in therapy have no intention to heal. Many people dispensing therapeutic advice have no commitment to their own healing. For these people, therapists and clients alike, therapy is a form of denial.

Letting the wound heal by itself is just as important as ministering to the wound. We forget that God, or the spiritual essence of the person, does the healing. It is not the therapist or healer who heals.

Those who intervene or interfere in the natural healing process will ultimately be called to account for the damage they do. For attack is attack under any guise. And the compulsion to heal is just as vicious as the compulsion to wound. They are different faces of the same coin.

The true healer respects the inner healing ability of her patient. She helps her patient make the connections that are ready to be made. She advocates integration, gentleness, patience. Thus, her clients get stronger. They heal and move on.

The unhealed healer is only too quick to make his patient into a victim, too quick to blame others. The false healer incarcerates his patient and takes away his freedoms.

The patient is stripped of all dignity and self-confidence. He is made dependent on drugs, machines, and doctor authority figures. What happens in some hospitals differs very little from what happens in the most vicious religious cults. It is a story of degradation and enslavement. To call it healing is preposterous if not obscene.

If you are not to make a mockery of the healing process, you must avoid the extremes of denial and fabrication of pain. Pain must be faced, not imagined. If it is there, it will express itself authentically. It will speak with its own voice. Your job is to invite the voice to speak, not to give it the words to say.

Scapegoating does little for anyone's healing. Overcoming shame is more important than finding people to blame. Even when it is clear that violation has occurred, punishing the perpetrator is not the solution. For the perpetrator is already a victim and punishing him just reinforces his own shame and powerlessness.

The question you must learn to ask is not "how do we heal?" But "how do we create a safe space where healing can occur?" If you can learn how to do that, then healing will take care of itself. And, in so doing, you will also be creating the environment in which the conditions that cause abuse will be undone at their roots.

Authenticity and Acceptance

Whatever your experience has been, your challenge is to learn to accept it, to be with it without judgment, to embrace it unconditionally. When you can do that, you can integrate the experience and the lessons it brings into the fabric of your life. Authenticity is the fruit of a life fully lived.

The denial or fabrication of experience is inauthentic and therefore unspiritual. It results in the fragmentation of consciousness, and the subjugation of one part of experience (unconscious) to another part (conscious). This creates an imbalance within the psyche that eventually needs to be healed. And healing invariably requires admitting the lie.

Telling the truth to oneself and others is the first requirement of the spiritual life. Without honesty, authenticity is impossible.

Telling the truth about what happened is necessary before the experience can be accepted and integrated. Secrets need to be disclosed.

If dissociation has occurred, one may have repressed the memory of what happened. Yet invariably, the memory will surface as one becomes capable of looking at it. One cannot and should not rush the process.

Don't deny what happened. Don't make it up. Just acknowledge what happened and be with it. That is what starts the shift from untruth to truth, from secrets to revelation, from hidden discomfort to the conscious awareness of pain.

Pain is a door you walk through when you are ready. Until then, you are the doorkeeper, the sentinel who stands guard and decides whom to exclude and whom to let in.

It is okay not to be ready. It's okay to exclude people or situations that feel unsafe. You are in charge of your own healing process. You decide how fast to go. Don't let anyone else dictate the pace of your healing process. It must be self-directed. If you work with a therapist/healer, he or she should be constantly checking with you to see if the process continues to feel safe to you.

Honoring your own process is essential to a life lived authentically. Others will always have ideas, suggestions, plans for you. Thank them for their concern, but be clear that you, not they, are making the decisions in your life.

Remember, low self esteem makes you a sitting duck for those whose particular form of self denial lies in preaching to others. Realize clearly and once and for all that anyone who thinks he knows more than you do about your life is nothing more than a thief posing as a healer. He has to rob others because he feels so insecure and lacking in himself.

Beware of those who criticize you "for your own good." And watch out when they play to your guilt. You don't owe anyone anything, except the truth.

"No," is not a bad thing to say when people invite you to betray yourself. Indeed, it is precisely what your experience is attempting to teach you.

Say "no" to all bargains and trades for love and approval. They cannot make you happy. Don't give away your freedom in return for a few conditional strokes.

You need your freedom if you are to learn to be yourself fully. A genuine spiritual guide celebrates your freedom and encourages you to follow your own heart. A true teacher points you within, where you receive your guidance, and not without. For guidance is never found through the concepts and opinions of others.

Permission to Betray

The majority of people you accept as authority figures in your life will abuse you. Your act of accepting their authority constitutes permission to them to abuse you. You may say "but I didn't know they would take advantage of me." And I say to you, brother or sister, "Wise up. Take responsibility for your life. Realize that you bought the farm. Stop trying to blame another for the choices you make."

You gave permission. Perhaps you did not know how bad it would be. The abuse came, as it frequently does, wrapped in sugar coated promises. Friendship may have been offered. Or financial security. Or companionship. Or sex. You name it. It doesn't matter what the bait was. You swallowed it and you got hooked. Be wiser next time. See the offer for what it is, an attempt to manipulate to gain love and approval.

Love cannot come from manipulation because the desire

to manipulate another comes from fear and insecurity. It may promise love, but it cannot deliver it.

Don't believe those who say they would sacrifice their good for yours. Even if it were true, they would be committing a sin against themselves and nothing good could come of it.

Don't accept anyone else's authority over you and don't accept authority over anyone else. Claim your freedom and offer freedom to others.

Those who try to manipulate or bargain for love will spend their whole lives in an emotional labyrinth with little hope of egress. Conditional love is an endless prison. The only escape is to tell the truth to yourself and others. Then you can walk free.

Neither a borrower nor a lender be. Do not borrow approval from others. Do not offer it when others seek it from you. Get out of the approval business. Get out of the lending business. Give what you can give with your whole heart and let the rest lie where it is.

Too many of you get caught in the horizontal journey. I have tried to tell you that, no matter how far you go in the exploration of "other," you will return to self. Earth is round. After you travel the circumference of the planet, you return to the same place.

Why leave self at all? Why go astray seeking the other when there is no other. There is only the self. This you will discover sooner or later. The more you go out the more you will return home.

All others offer you a detour from the universe of self. The more you believe that you need others to be happy the more miserable you will be. Happiness cannot be given by others, for, contrary to appearances, there are no others out there. There is only the self disguised as other. And in that disguise, self seems to be vicious indeed. It commits murder, rape, child abuse, you name it. It does all this because it believes itself to be other. It does all this in a desperate attempt to end separation by force.

It can't be done. Separation cannot be undone through force. The unloved cannot find love. Only the one whose heart is softening can find the love that stands before him. And the heart softens, not in reference to any other, but only through gentle acceptance of self.

Love yourself well and you can bring others into that love without difficulty. In truth, when two people meet who love self, there is no other present. There are just two who dwell in the single heart of love.

There is only one person here who needs to give and receive love and that is you. Give love to yourself and include others in that love. If they do not wish to be included, let them go. It is no loss. You do not need another detour, another useless journey.

Be steadfast in your love for yourself. Let that be your absolute number one commitment. Grace will bring others in who are happy to be with themselves. They will not come in making demands of you. They will not come in trying to take control of your life.

When someone makes you an offer you can't refuse, you must learn to refuse it. Don't betray yourself, regardless of the price.

The tempter will always come to you offering extraordinary gifts. Don't be fooled. He seems to have supernatural powers, but they are not real. He is just your brother moving off course, trying to draw you into his drama of self-abuse.

Don't say yes to his abuse or yours. Put God first. God tells you: "Your needs are completely met. You are whole. You lack nothing. Relax and breathe. This too will pass."

But the tempter shouts out: "No. You are not okay. You are lonely. You need companionship. You need a better job. You need a better relationship. You need more money, more sex, more notoriety; all of this will I give to you."

Surely, you have heard this pitch before! Some knight in shining armor or damsel in distress always appears when you are feeling low. Where has it gotten you in the past? How many knights or damsels have sped off on their steeds leaving a trail of blood and tears?

Yet this one seems better than the last. He or she is more sincere, more sensitive, more grounded. You fill in the words. It is your drama, not mine.

If you look deeply enough, you will see that every pitch is the same. Every invitation to self-betrayal has the same sugar coated promises and the same heart-wrenching core.

Those who seek salvation in another bring otherness in. They lose touch with self.

They go off like Quixote on the great horizontal journey. And they always find damsels to rescue and windmills to fight. That's part of the terrain.

But in the end, they return home tired, wounded, and lacking in faith. The horizontal journey defeats everyone who takes it. There is no salvation to be found in the world. There is no doing that leads to peace.

What leads to peace is beyond doing. You can find it only if you stay at home. Stay with the self. Bring love to the parts of the self that still feel unloved. Become rooted in the eternal blessing of God's abundance and grace.

All who meet you here come bringing genuine gifts. Here there are no strings attached, no neurotic bargaining for love and approval. Here there is authentic wholeness, the joy of being present alone and together. Here abuse is impossible, for there is no other to distract the self and take it from its purpose. Here freedom and love are intertwined, because each supports the other. Here there is only self.

Emerging from the Dream

All apparent abuse is a game between phantoms or shadows. People emerge with gaping wounds. They appear to get hurt, but genuine hurt is impossible, because the self is unassailable. You cannot put holes in it. You can only pretend to hurt or be hurt.

Nobody can be separated from the source of love, but

174

people believe that they can be, and their actions are based on this belief. As soon as this belief is challenged, love reveals itself. For it is always there behind the drama of attack and defense.

If we see only the surface of what happens in life, we will see through a glass darkly. We will see only dream images. But if we lift the curtain and look behind it, we will see the actors behind the persona. We will see how everything that happens to us is called for from the depths of our being.

And everything we call for contributes to our awakening. It forces us to look behind the curtain. It forces us to drop our roles of victim or victimizer. It exposes our secrets and lets us know "they are no big deal." It lets us know that nothing can separate us from love, because we are love incarnate. We are the shining ones dreaming the dream of abuse. We are the angels walking as wounded.

Denying our hurts doesn't take us home. Pretending to be angels when we feel like abused kids does not contribute to our awakening. But neither does holding onto the wound.

When the wound is addressed with love, it heals. That healing can be instantaneous or it can take a lifetime, depending on the degree of our surrender to love. But victimization does stop and healing does happen. The drama of suffering does comes to an end.

Awakening is not a wrenching process, but a gentle giving up of blame and shame. A gentle letting go of projection.

It is not that love makes the bad go away, but that all perceptions of bad fade away in the presence of love. All woundedness dissolves in love's embrace. And in the end, it is as if the wound never happened. At best, you could say it was a dream of abuse, a dream from which we have gloriously awakened.

I who was crucified can tell you that you too will be lifted from your cross, full bodied and whole. You were never injured by your experience. Nobody was ever able to take from you anything that genuinely belonged to you.

Only your illusions have been stripped away from you. And for that you will be thankful, even as I am thankful to my executioners for helping me remove the last vestiges of ignorance from my soul.

Who you are is inseparable from love. It is therefore inevitable that you will awaken from the dream of separation. It is inevitable that you will take your rightful place at my side.

Nothing that you can do will change this outcome. God made certain of this.

You cannot hurt yourself permanently. You cannot cut yourself off permanently from God's love. At best, you can take a circular journey away from yourself. At best, you can be seduced into thinking that happiness or unhappiness lies outside of you.

But you will be abused of that notion, for abuse is correction. And like any correction, it brings you back on course. When you see that what you once perceived of as attack was merely a correction for your own waywardness, it is not difficult to forgive yourself or your abuser. Both of you were calling out for correction. Each was for the other a voice in the wilderness, an answer to the call for love.

Solitude

Your fear of being alone and your emotional dependency on others set you up for many disappointments. Constant failure in relationships exacerbates old wounds, making it harder for them to heal. Self confidence is diminished and anxiety about one's self worth and capacity for relationship are increased.

All this can be shifted if you are willing to accept your aloneness as a state of being. Define your life so that it serves you, so that it makes room for activities that you enjoy and relationships that honor you and respect your boundaries. Find a way to care for your body and express your creativity. Live in an inspirational place. Find quiet time to center yourself. Walk in the woods or by the ocean. Work at something you enjoy doing. Be joyful. Eat well. Sleep well. Refine the quality of your life. Care about yourself.

Caring about yourself is a full time vocation. Do not try to make it into a part time activity. It must become the one major focus of your life. Otherwise, you are accepting a different purpose for your life, one that is not consistent with your peace and happiness.

When you become established in the flow of your life and your days are full of joy, creativity, and caring for self and others, you will be naturally guided into relationships that honor your newfound energy, optimism, and tranquility. These relationships will be different from any you have experienced so far, because they will have a foundation of self-caring to build on.

When both people know how to take care of themselves and enjoy doing so, there is no mutual invitation to self-betrayal. One does not expect the other to care for him or her.

The relationship promises one nothing other than what one has. It is enriching and expansive, but not in any sense necessary. One does not need the relationship to feel loved and cared for, because that is a gift one has already given to oneself.

Solitude is necessary for your emotional health, whether you are living alone or living with another. Solitude gives you the time and space to integrate your experience. And all growth depends on integration.

Having lots of experiences means nothing if you do not take the time to learn from them and make that learning part of the operating code for your life. Jumping from activity to activity or relationship to relationship wreaks havoc on the emotional core of the person. With such disturbance in the emotional body, equanimity and bliss are impossible and life becomes empty of spirit.

Without solitude, spiritual nourishment will be lacking. If you want a single cause for the amount of distress in the world, it is the fact that people do not take time to commune with self, nature and the divine. A spiritual life — a life free of needless tension and self-created suffering — requires such communion.

If you keep the Sabbath, you dedicate one day a week for self-nurturing and God communion. That is enough to keep you centered in your life. If you meditate or take a long silent walk for an hour each day, you can achieve the same goal. It doesn't matter what ritual you choose, as long as it provides time for silent reflection.

The time you take to integrate your experience is as important as the time you take to have the experience itself. If you remember that, you will assimilate your lessons with greater depth and rapidity.

If you eat a meal and then take a half hour nap, you will wake up rejuvenated. You will have given your body uninterrupted time to work on digestion. Try to do the same thing with all of your experiences. Allow time for digestion and assimilation. Let your experience percolate within you. Be with it. Let it live inside you, before you try to respond or live out from it.

Every breath you take has three movements: an inhale, a pause, and an exhale. The inhale is for the taking in of experience. The pause is for its assimilation. And the exhale is for the release of experience. While the pause is just a second or two, it is essential for the integrity of the breath.

Likewise, solitude is essential for the conscious, integrated experience of life. Quality of life rests on it. Energy and spirituality rest on it.

If you drop out this part, your life will be an empty shell. A great deal may pass in and out of it. But nothing will stick. There will be no growth in consciousness.

Rhythm

The simple beauty and majesty of life is to be found in its cyclical rhythms: the rising and setting of the sun, the phases of the moon, the changes in the seasons, the beating of the heart, the rhythmic unfolding of the breath. Repetition provides continuity, familiarity, safety. Yet within every cycle, there are variations that provide challenges and opportunities for growth.

Many people now are disconnected from the rhythms of nature and their own bodies. As a result, they do not experience a safe, nurturing, context in which to live their lives and integrate the challenges that arise. This is one of the tragedies of contemporary life. There is very little to count on.

The connection with the earth, the physical body, the breath, is disrupted. The extended family is non-existent. The nuclear family is attenuated if not defunct. Life today is a shell of what it used to be.

Changes happen perpetually without the time to reflect on them and integrate them. Relationships begin and end before people can establish any kind of interpersonal flow. Emotional demands crater the landscape of the heart, tearing into the soft tissue. Trust is maimed, patience forgotten.

Everyone today is a walking wounded. Yet few notice it. Life goes on, driven to perpetual distraction. As entertainment flourishes, awareness and communion wane. More and more stimuli intrude. Life becomes busyness. The only quiet time is during sleep, and even that is prey to restless dreams.

This is what you call life, yet it is a travesty of life. It is life without breath, without energy, without intimacy. It is an attack on the senses, an overwhelming of the mind, a violation of the spirit.

It is life without heart, without rhythm.

Life without rhythm is ungrounded. It reaches for the heavens while ignoring the earth. It spins out, careening wildly thorough the sky, moving from one self-destructive adventure to another. It is unsafe and abusive to all concerned.

The more unsafe it seems, the more the wounded child inside seeks the security it believes an authority figure can provide. But that is just a trap. The greater one's need for outside approval, the more devastating the betrayal of trust will be.

People marry authority figures. They elect them. They go to their churches and join their cults. Yet, gradually, all these authority figures will be discredited. And, as they fall from their pedestals, those who worshiped them will move in for the kill. It is an old story.

You live in a time when all external authority will be undermined and abolished. The more people look without, the more their lessons will force them to look within. That is the awakening.

That is the time in which you live.

All who seek the sky without getting roots in the earth will be beat up by their experiences. In time they will return, shovels in hand, and begin the work of planting.

There are no wings without roots, except for birds. And they make sure to take shelter in trees with deep roots in the ground.

All that is spinning out to heaven will fall to earth, abused, shattered, forsaken, licking its imagined wounds. That which is rootless will learn to grow roots. That which has sought authority without will learn to find it within.

And then, with feet firmly planted in the earth, the eyes will notice the procession of sun and the moon. The senses feel the rise of sap in the spring and the lifting of leaves in the fall. Blood and breath will be restored. Rhythm will return. Safety will be re-created where it authentically lies, in the heart of each person. And organic order will be re-established on earth.

If you are not growing roots, you are asking for trouble. Only your own rootedness can help you bring heaven to earth. Not willfulness or spiritual pride. Not left brained agendas.

Spirituality is a living with, not a living for. It is the poetry of being, the rhythm of life unfolding in each person, each relationship, each community.

Part 9

Embracing Self

Committing to Self

Most of you know what you want, but you do not wait for it. You are constantly compromising your needs and your values to fit the situations which present themselves to you. You take the job or the relationship not because it offers you what you desire, but because you are afraid a better offer won't come. You live your life afraid to take risks because you do not want to give up the security you have.

I have news for you. That security is your death knell. It prevents you from asking sincerely for what you want.

If you are ready to release negative, masochistic, people-pleasing patterns, you must be willing to stand in the conviction of who you are, no matter how others respond to you. You must reach down deeply inside yourself and affirm yourself as you alone know yourself to be.

Put the ideas and opinions of others aside and stand in your own integrity. Step fully into your thoughts and feelings. Inhabit your life. Connect with your joy. Find the source of energy and wisdom in yourself, and live out from that center.

Lest you take the time to do this, you will not connect with your own desire energy. You cannot reach out and take hold of life if you are always apologizing for yourself or seeking to win the approval of others.

Take the time to breathe and connect. Take the time to be, find your joy, and commit to it. Stop looking without. Take a day, a week or a month and look within.

Make a commitment to yourself. How else can you find the self?

You require your attention!

Your thoughts and feelings require validation from you.

For a moment, stop looking for satisfaction outside yourself. Do what makes you happy. Do not question it or apologize for it.

Care for yourself gently and generously.

Eat what you want to eat. Sleep as long as you want to. Energize yourself on all levels of your being.

Do not compromise. Be committed to you.

Do it for one hour a day, every day without fail. Or do it one day per week every week without fail. Give this time to yourself as a gift.

This is how you become acquainted with yourself. This is how you develop a commitment to you.

Without a commitment to yourself, nothing worthwhile can be accomplished in life. If you have never committed to yourself, how can you commit to another?

You can't!

There are millions of people who think that they are in committed relationships, yet very few of them have committed to themselves. Most of them have used their "commitment" to another to avoid committing to themselves.

Does self-commitment seem selfish to you?

If so, you must learn that what honors you cannot possibly hurt or take anything away from others. If others feel disturbed by your commitment to yourself, you may take this as a sign that they are actively betraying themselves. How could they possibly empower you? Their opinions and agendas will always take you away from yourself.

Don't be a fool and give your time and attention here. People who betray themselves seek to manipulate others because they believe that others have something to offer them that they can't get from themselves. Of course, this is not true.

Others can offer you only what you can give to yourself, because they are simply the reflection of that. Everything that you can get from another is already present within yourself or you would not be able to call that reflection to you.

The perception that others can give or take away from the self is an illusion. No one can give you what you do not have or take away what you do have. Only what is illusory can be given or taken away. Only judgment, interpretation, opinion and approval can be given and taken away. If you accept these false gifts to prop up your self confidence, be prepared for the time when they are wrested away.

To accept a false gift from another is to betray the self. It is to place value on what is without value. If you build on quicksand, do not be surprised if your house is destroyed in the first storm.

You have only two choices in life. You can be faithful to self or you can betray the self. No one else is responsible for your happiness or lack of it.

In betraying yourself, you betray others, for all self-betrayal is insincere and dishonest. When you do not ask for what you want and/or when you accept what you do not want, you set others up for disappointment. Sooner or later, you will have to admit the truth: you don't really want what you asked for!

All abuse emanates from the initial lie we tell ourselves. The lie is: I want you, when the truth is I want myself. If you accept this lie, you will try in vain to give me myself, but it will never work. You can never give me myself unless I am willing to give me myself. If I am using my relationship with you to avoid myself, then there is absolutely no way you can give me what I want.

In such cases, it will be only a matter of time before my illusory desire for you runs its course and it becomes clear to me that you cannot give me what I want. If I am particularly scared of meeting myself, I will continue to seek self through others, leaving a wake of false promises and unnecessary tears. It is not that I consciously abuse you. It is that my decision not to honor myself leads to a cul de sac. I seek self through other and self cannot be found there. If you join me on that journey, you can be sure that you too are seeking self through other. And your outcome will be the same as mine. What we promise to each other cannot not be given. Our relationship is a set-up for both of us. We are mirrors for each other.

The cycle of abuse continues until you wake up. Waking

up means not projecting blame onto the other person. It means refusing to be a victim. It means seeing your own self-betrayal for what it is.

When you let the other off the hook and acknowledge the self-betrayal, you will take the first step toward breaking this abusive pattern. That step is merely to see that your search for the beloved in another is a futile search. The more you look without for love, the more adamantly you are brought face to face with yourself.

I have said before that until you meet the beloved within, you cannot meet him or her without. Others can give you only what you are willing to give yourself. And what you are unwilling to give — which of course is what you want — cannot be given by another.

Does this mean that all relationships constitute a betrayal of self and are doomed to failure? Not all perhaps, but far more than you think!

Most relationships are a conspiracy on behalf of both partners to avoid making a commitment to themselves. They use the other person as a substitute for genuine surrender to the presence of love within.

The only way out of the detour of co-dependent, mutually deceptive relationships is to befriend the self, honor the self, love and embrace the self. Then one can build relationship on the truth of self-coherence. This is the new paradigm of relationship.

In the new paradigm, my commitment to love you is always an extension of my commitment to love myself. Because I love you, my commitment to self is extended to include you. I am therefore committed to both of us at the same time.

In the old paradigm relationship, the commitment to self is vitiated by the commitment to other. In seeking to please the other, self is abandoned. Since the abandoned self is incapable of love, this constitutes a vicious cycle of attraction and rejection. First the self is excluded, and then the other is excluded.

All genuine relationship must be built on the foundation of one's acceptance of and love for self. That is the primary spiritual gesture, the one that opens the door to the potential for intimacy.

When you know what you want you can ask for it. When someone says "I'm sorry. I can't offer you that," you say "No problem. It will come in good time." You stay focused on what you want, regardless of what people offer you. You reject all the conditions with which love and attention are offered to you. You hold fast to the truth of your heart, accepting no less than you have promised to yourself.

And, in time, it comes, because you have been faithful to yourself, because you have learned to bring love to yourself. Because you have answered the call within your own heart, the Beloved appears unannounced at your doorstep. This is not a magical formula, but the fruit of a committed spiritual practice.

Illumination

The world you know is engendered by self-betrayal. It is a sad, defeated, spiritless world. Those who try to redeem it do so by focusing on the betrayal of others, legislating victimhood and making attack a crime. They do not know that the only attack is self attack. And if you punish someone for attacking himself, it just perpetuates the pattern of abuse.

Instead of exploring the wound and finding its cause within the psyche, the responsibility for the wound is projected on another. A scapegoat is found. Another lamb is led to the slaughter because a human being did not have the strength and the courage to look within.

As long as you try to make the object responsible for the subject's behavior, you will fulfill the dictum of "an eye for an eye." This will not bring peace to you or others.

Do you truly believe that anyone can be a victim or a

victimizer without betraying the self? That is not possible. All abuse is self abuse, whether you are the apparent giver or receiver of it.

Why, I ask you, do you have more compassion for the victim than you do for the victimizer? Is it not because you do not see the victimizer also as a victim? Or because you do not see the victim also as a victimizer?

Redemption cannot be experienced so long as you see either victim or victimizer as object, as other. Both are subject. Both are self.

Both are self seeking itself through other. Both are betraying the self.

Both victim and victimizer call out to each other. And when they answer the call, they do so with conviction. Thanks to the other, each is given a wake up call. Each is shown the self-betrayal, if only he or she will look.

As a compassionate society, we should help people to look and to take responsibility. We must do this with profound gentleness and compassion. We do not want to "blame the victim" or "condone the actions of the perpetrator." We simply want each one to use the opportunity to learn more deeply to honor self.

All social problems come from the dishonoring of self. Yet the dishonoring of self is not addressed in your schools or churches. The most important subject is not taught.

Perhaps that is because you do not understand it yourself. But that is changing. The time when the symptom receives more attention than the cause is coming to an end. As symptoms proliferate and become untreatable, attention will automatically shift to addressing the cause of dis-ease.

As long as you are afraid to look at the darkness, the light will not come. As long as you deny the self by seeking it through another, you will have trespass and abuse. If you want love, bring love to the places in yourself that feel unloved. If you want light, bring it to the dark places of your mind. Bring it to the fear and the shame, to the sadness, to the perceived lack of purpose or hope.

That light is within you. It is not separate from the darkness. It is a quality of the darkness itself. When you get to absolute pitch blackness, there illumination is found. Blackest black becomes radiant. Sadness turns to unaccountable joy. Despair turns to hope without measure. In one pole, you will find the other. Venture into the darkness and the light will be revealed. Go into the light and the shadows will emerge.

Both light and shadow are necessary. To go beyond duality, you must experience it fully. You must see how each pole abides in and is connected to its opposite. You must appreciate the cyclical play of energies.

As long as you think reality is linear and sequential, you will encounter events and circumstances which appear totally discontinuous with your experience. They aren't discontinuous, but they appear to be, based on the way that you look at them.

When you dwell in the heart of your conflict and confusion, you move through the limits of linear thinking. You see that reality is circular, that the inner and outer are in constant dialogue and that everything that happens is a mirror.

If you can be in this space without needing to define it or explain it — without bringing the linear mind back in — you can successfully remove the veil of projection and interpretation and directly commune with your experience as it unfolds. When that happens, you stop asking "what does this mean?" and just rest in the inherent meaning. Without verbal and conceptual filters interfering, that meaning can unfold energetically in one's life. In this manner, one moves spontaneously out of difficulty and struggle without necessarily knowing how or why.

The primary shift that occurs here is a withdrawal of attention from object-oriented perception. We cease to make others responsible in any way for our experience. We notice what others do or don't do, but we refrain from interpreting it. We place our attention instead on witnessing our own thoughts and feelings moment to moment. We watch our judgments and interpretations and see how they give rise to various feeling states, and how those states invoke memories and past perceptions.

We observe without trying to figure anything out. We just stay with our experience. And gradually we find that we are more present and centered in each moment. The pace of our life slows down, because we stop trying to make things happen.

Our relationship to ourself and our experience shifts. We are no longer the one who needs "to do" our life. We don't have to bring our timetables and agendas. All that can go. Now, we are simply the one who wishes "to be with" our experience.

In other words, we stop putting gas in the tank and the car eventually runs out of gas. We stop making new projections and our remaining projections eventually run their course. We stop seeking ourselves in others and we connect with the self we need to find.

None of this happens in a linear way. There are two steps backwards for every step forward. Yet, contrary to what you might believe, this is progress. Every step forward is worth one hundred steps back. That is the nature of the learning process. Every time you embrace truth, years of false beliefs are released.

Alone, with Heart Open

When you finally discover that no one else can betray you, your relationship to your brother changes profoundly. He is no longer someone who can hurt you or treat you unfairly. Nor is he someone who can save you or make you feel better about yourself.

Because you don't worship him or scapegoat him, his significance in your life greatly diminishes. He is simply a fellow traveler, a neighbor. You are willing to help him from time to time or receive his help. But you no longer wish to depend on him or have him become dependent on you.

A new and healthy sense of boundaries is established in all of your relationships. You become capable of being a friend and receiving the fruits of friendship from others. But your interest in your brother or sister is no longer intrusive. Your happiness does not depend on how he or she responds to you.

The more you become established in yourself, the more you take your brothers and sisters off the hook. They no longer have to be perfect in your eyes. You see their shortcoming and mistakes without judging them harshly. You see their beauty and integrity without envy or the need to possess.

The more you claim your freedom to be yourself, the easier it becomes for you to grant others the same freedom. You do not demand attention from others, nor do you seek relationships which would make artificial demands on your time or attention.

When you are alone, you remain open to others. When you are with someone, you are not thrown off center.

Since you offer what you have freely to others, you never lack for company. Nor on the other hand do you require company for a sense of completion.

Thus, your aloneness deepens your connection with the self without closing your heart. You stay open and receptive to others, without being drawn into their dramas of self-abuse.

Marriage Vs Celibacy

Establishing in the self is the true meaning of celibacy. It has nothing per se to do with sexual abstinence. You can be sexually active and still be celibate, provided their is no compulsion or deception in your sexual activity.

When you are celibate, you do not promise anyone an

exclusive partnership. Your vow is to honor yourself and tell the truth in each moment. If you sleep with someone today, it does not necessarily mean that you want to live with that person. It does not necessarily mean that you want to sleep with that person exclusively. It simply means that you are present physically and emotionally with that person in the moment. And you are committed to exploring the relationship as it evolves without trying to put your life together with the other person.

A celibate person is not looking for marriage. He or she is committed to being single as a spiritual path. Being single might mean not having sex with anyone or it might mean having sex with one or more consenting partners.

Since most people require some kind of commitment when they are sexual together, sexual activity tends to be more safely confined to marriage or some other committed ongoing relationship. However, obviously, for some people, this commitment is not a very deep or long lasting one. Many married people engage in affairs, spouse swapping, pornography, or sexual activity outside the marriage. This just tends to underscore the fact that fidelity to another is impossible without fidelity to self.

Celibate people consciously choose a lifestyle of living alone. They are up front with prospective partners about their decision not to marry or live with one person. They choose to live alone because their creative pursuits and/or spiritual practices require the majority of their time and attention and make living full time with another person an unwise and unwieldy proposition.

There is nothing wrong or right with celibacy. It is one spiritual path. Marriage is another. Both paths have their challenges and their rewards. Moreover, during the course of one's lifetime, one may choose to be married first, then celibate, or celibate first, then married. Such choices are progressive. Society would do well to acknowledge the importance of different interpersonal models as people go through the inevitable lifecycle changes.

Of all the choices available, abstinence is the least likely to succeed. It is tragic that the church has demanded this sacrifice of its clergy. Very few people are capable of sexual abstinence. Those who try and find that they cannot do it must engage in secretive, deceptive, abusive behavior in order to satisfy themselves and maintain their position. Witness the many cases of pedophilia and other sexual assault that have undermined the authority of the clergy in your time.

It is time that such abuses come to light. And it is time that all religions rethink their positions on both celibacy and abstinence. For a clergyperson may in good faith choose to be married — being a model to the congregation of what a successful marriage looks like — or to be single and celibate — being a model to the flock of the life of a solitary visionary or mystic.

As you begin to better understand the essence of celibacy, new options will be created for people who are attracted to this way of life. New monasteries will be created where men and women can live together in a non-traditional lifestyle in service to God.

In the end, the form your life takes does not matter as much as your commitment to honesty and truth. An honest but unconventional life is to be greatly preferred to a traditional life twisted by secrets and lies.

When form does not express the spirit that inhabits it, it becomes a prison. Almost every institution in your world, both religious and secular, has become restrictive and pernicious. Better to let the form go while the essence can still be salvaged. Better to align with spirit and rebuild the form creatively and cooperatively than to let spirit die out because of lack of vision.

In case you had doubts, let me tell you, there is plenty of work to do. Lest you thought there was no particular purpose for your life, let me remind you that wherever you feel pain, constriction or struggle, there does your purpose unfold. Because you choose to honor yourself, the world will change. That is the promise of your life. May you awaken to it and fulfill it with enthusiasm, dignity and self-respect.

Creativity and Conformity

No one tells you that you have to conform to the values and standards of the dominant reality around you, yet conform you do. Your great desire in life is to fit in with others and be accepted by them. Even if you are expressing yourself creatively in an authentic way, you still care about what other people think. You still want people to buy your books or your paintings. You still need to make a living.

Abundance thinking doesn't help you pay the bills. By promising immediate and spectacular results, it sets you up for disappointment.

When you move across the grain, you can expect more friction than when you don't. When you challenge the values, standards and perceptions of dominant reality, you can't expect to be supported financially by it.

Original work breaks new ground. And the more faithful you are to your own creative vision, the more you will tend to move off into uncharted territory. A true artist — and each one of us is a true artist if we will honor ourselves — is ahead of her time. She does not act from the outside in. She does not make her work conform to the demands and expectations of the marketplace. And so she claims a freedom that each of you must eventually claim: the freedom to be and express yourself fully.

However, self-expression by itself is only half of the picture. One can be truly creative but have a heart that is shut down. Self expression without feedback is solipsistic. It is not a dialogue with anyone. It does not attempt to communicate. Without communication and dialogue, creative work does not grow. It turns in on itself. It becomes a private language. It is a kind of mental masturbation.

The extremes of artistic license and artistic conformity are to be avoided. The former closes the audience out. The latter closes the artist in.

Don't be foolish and expect your creative endeavors to speak to others if you don't use a vernacular language. It you want to engage others and communicate, you must speak in a language that people understand.

This does not mean that you tailor your work to some abstract expectation you think others have of it. That would tie your creative process in knots. You do your work so that it speaks to your heart. You speak plainly and directly, the way you would like to be spoken to.

There is no pose, no artifice, no stance in your work. There is no pretension to be what you are not. There is simply the genuine desire to share your experience.

Will authentic work support you? Perhaps it will. Perhaps it won't.

In an enlightened society, all authentic work would be supported. But the world you live in has not reached that point of trust and investment in the creative process.

What you cannot afford to do is to deny the creative aspect of your being just because it does not support you financially. That is self-betrayal.

Find a way to make time and space for your creative self-expression. Give yourself an hour a day, or a day a week. Make a consistent commitment to your own creative process. Let there be a rhythm with it. Make it a ritual of self-honoring. Build it into the structure of your life.

Self expression is essential to the honoring of self. One must not only take time to integrate one's experience, but to respond to it as well. And the response is one's invitation to dialogue with others. It is the gesture that builds community.

No one is meant to be isolated. Yet everyone is meant to express himself honestly. The desire for approval prevents honest self-expression. It is soft and apologetic. The flip side of this is the need to shock. It is often harsh and offensive, pushing people away. Both are aspects of the search for approval, and are made in anticipation of the response of others.

Authentic expression is neither offensive nor apologetic. It states its point simply and invites dialogue. It builds bridges between people's various perceptions of experience. It stimulates growth and intimacy.

Without the full realization of the creativity of each person, social life becomes dull, humdrum, restrictive and boring. It caves in upon itself. There is no spark, no energy, no diversity or interchange.

A family or educational system that does not foster creativity and teamwork is not doing its job. In an enlightened society, children are encouraged to honor their creative process and respect that of others. Time and space are provided for individual self-directed work, as well as for sharing and cooperative group activities.

If you want to improve life for your children, start by honoring your own creative process and by supporting them and your partner in honoring theirs. Do not become lost in the "busyness" of living. Set aside times to honor the self and times to share the fruits of reflection and self-expression.

The more you trust your creative process and endeavor to support that of others, the more you will be helping to create the conditions for a sane and loving world. Increasingly, as you commit to the ritual of self honoring, you will see that support for your process is established in your life.

This kind of support is not built overnight, notwithstanding the promises of the prophets of abundance. It evolves over time as the commitment to self takes root and reaches deeply into the ground of being.

As always, actions speak louder than words. Unless you follow through on what you believe, it will have little significance in your life.

Part 10

Awareness

The Wounded Angel

Wounds are illusions that must be corrected. The trick is not to deny the wound, but to bring love to it. When awareness of the unwounded whole (love) is brought to the wounded part (unloved), the wound disappears.

Victims need wounds to uphold their victimhood. The attachment to pain and hurt is a condition of the perception of self as a victim. When self is no longer seen as a victim, there is no more attachment to pain. Pain may come and go. But one does not find any meaning in it.

The self cannot be damaged by its experience. All experience contributes to reawakening the memory of the one self: absolute, all-inclusive and therefore unassailable.

Because of the division into bodies, it appears that there is more than one self and that each has its own destiny. However, in truth, there is only one self and one destiny. To discover the one self in oneself, one must surrender to the uniqueness of one's life experience. One must claim one's own authentic process and journey.

The more one individuates, the closer one comes to touching the universal experience. All who touch the universal experience by walking through the door of self, fall directly into the heart. They no longer have to talk about love or forgiveness. They are the essence of love and forgiveness.

This should indicate to you the utter futility of following someone else's ideas or using their experience to validate your own. Only by accepting what comes directly and experientially to you will you find the door to the universal.

It is paradoxical perhaps. To encounter the universal, you must fully individuate. What appears to be selfish actually brings wholeness. And wholeness is the door to the one self. All teachings of self-abnegation are false. To go beyond the small self, you must become it fully. You must inhabit it and break through it.

Do not deny yourself experience. That will just inhibit your progress. Reach out and embrace every aspect of your experience. That is the engine that takes you to the end of the tracks.

If you want to come into your angelhood, you must learn to be completely human, completely authentic, completely present and open to your experience. Angels are not seven foot creatures with wings. They are beings who have learned to honor themselves. Because they have walked through the door, they can hold the door open for you.

Don't see angels outside of yourself. That is not where they will be found. They live in a dimension that you can touch only through your heart. To call to them is to call yourself at the deepest level.

Your presence as an angelic being manifests as you wake from the dream of self-abuse. You remember, as Satan does, that you used to stand with God. Since then, out of your own willfulness, you have fallen from grace. You have tried to manage your life without spirit at the helm. Now you know that it doesn't work. Now your fall is broken and you begin the journey back to God.

But first you must release all your hatred toward yourself, all your feelings of failure. First, you must let go of all that you think you are. You are not a bad person because you made mistakes, however heavily those misdeeds may weigh on your conscience. You are simply the one who tried to act independently before you were ready. You left home prematurely and you got into trouble.

Take heart. You have loving parents. Come home. Tell them that leaving was a mistake, that you weren't prepared to take on the challenges of the world. They will understand. They will welcome you back. And when you feel you are ready to leave again, they will not hold you back.

Who can hold back the chain of being? Who can stop you from leaving home and moving into embodiment? It is not possible to defray the hunger for experience. It will always have its way.

You come into this world thinking it will be easy but it is anything but that. What seemed to be a gentle walk up the hill of judgment turns into an intensely challenging climb. Sometimes you think you can't make it. So you give up too early. You bail out of the experience. Perhaps you even blow your brains out! But it doesn't help. Wherever you leave the path is where you will have to resume your journey. There are no shortcuts. No way to skip over the lessons you carefully fashioned for your awakening.

Reincarnation et al

Reincarnation, as it commonly is understood, does not exist. All incarnations are simultaneous. All dreams of self are present in this dream. That is why it is not helpful to concern yourself with who you were in some past life, unless memories spontaneously come up for your attention. There are no past lives, any more than there are past experiences.

The belief in the past is what limits your ability to be fully present in the moment. And that presence is necessary if you are to wake up from the dream of self-abuse.

In any moment you can be free of the past or enslaved by it. In any moment, you can be justifying your fear or walking through it.

Do not go in search of memories from the past. If they come up, acknowledge them, be with them and integrate them. Do this not to empower the past, but to complete it, so that you can be present now.

Anything that takes you away from your immediate communion with life is not helpful. On the other hand, resisting something that wants to come up takes you even further away from being present in the moment.

The concept of "past" is simply that: a concept. A way of describing experience as linear, sequential, causal. That is not the nature of experience. That is simply a commonly held description of it..

In truth, the past does not exist. It once existed as a present phenomenon, but it is present no longer, except to the degree that you hold onto it. If you are keeping the past present, then it must be dealt with now. Otherwise, it can be released. Once it is released, it no longer exists in consciousness. When it is released, you don't even remember that it happened.

If you don't remember that it happened, did it happen? "Yes," you will say, but that is because you are looking at it historically. Remember the question: if a tree falls in the forest and nobody hears it, did it make a sound?

The answer is no. Without an experiencer, there is no experience.

That is why self-forgiveness works. When the experiencer ceases to relive the experience, the experience ceases to exist. And he or she returns to the present innocent and unabused.

Are there past lives? Only if you remember them. And if you remember them, you will continue to live them until you come to forgiveness of yourself.

The key to all of this is simple: do not gather wood unless you want to make a fire. Do not stir the pot unless you want to smell the stew. Do not solicit the past unless you want to dance with it.

But if there is a fire in your house, you must pick up your things and leave. If the stew is boiling, you can't help but smell it. If the past is dancing in your mirror, you can't pretend to be in samadhi.

Resistance of experience creates endless detours. But so does seeking.

Do not resist. Do not seek. Just deal with what comes up as it arises.

Don't try to save the world. Don't try to save others. Don't try to save yourself. All that is seeking. All that just adds to your job description.

Do not be born. Do not go to school. Do not get married. Do not have children. Do not take a job. Do not get sick. Do not die.

If you have a choice, do not do it. Do not seek outside yourself.

But if you are born, if you go to school, get married, have children, take a job, get sick and die, then do it as consciously as you can. Learn as much as you can from each experience. Embrace it.

Because if you try to resist your experience, it will kick you in the derriere!

Nobody comes into embodiment with an empty plate. Everyone has at least a scrap or two to digest. (Some have seven course meals! But I'm not going to point any fingers, are you?)

Don't be discouraged by this. Since each person must deal with what's on his plate, let him deal with it as happily as he can.

Don't interfere in the lives of others or you will have a second or a third helping to dispose of. Stay detached from what someone else does or does not do. Don't even have an opinion about it. Just let it be.

When someone invites you to dinner, go and sit with him, but don't eat. Tell him you are fasting, or, if you must eat, bring your own food.

Don't borrow someone else's experience. Don't try to give someone else your experience.

Do you really think you are going to get credit for cleaning your plate if someone else does it for you?

To go beyond co-dependency, step into your life. Sleep in your own bed. Prepare your own food. Clean up after yourself. Practice taking care of yourself and let others do the same for themselves.

Past lives? Angels? UFOs? Astrology?

Give me a break! Give yourself a break!

Don't waste your time in this embodiment trying to give intellectual meaning and context to your experience. That is not your job. Your job is just to be present with your experience. So stop seeking. Stop resisting. Step into your life and live it as fully and as magnificently as you can. Then, I assure you, I will be your biggest cheerleader.

Belief Systems

Nothing will crucify you faster than your own thoughts. Better not to think at all, if you can do it.

And if you can't, if you must think, think about simple things. Think about washing the dishes or doing the laundry. Think about things that must be done. And then let the mind be free of thought.

Everything you believe about the nature of your existence keeps you limited to the past. If you want to experience the moment unconditionally, give up all your concepts of it. Just be present in your life as it unfolds.

Watch the tendency of the mind to try to figure everything out. Watch how it tries to structure and plan. Even when experience invalidates all the mentation about it, watch the mind go into revising, plotting and replotting. Watch it try to hold onto mutual exclusive possibilities. Watch how easily it goes into opposition and conflict.

Mind is always looking for the thread of the story so it can continue to weave the plot, or at least maintain the illusion of control. But the interesting thing is that there is no plot. Or, if there is a plot, the experiencer is part of it so he can't possibly see what the plot is.

The observer only knows himself through what he observes. He can't see what's not there. That is the inevitable limitation of manifest existence.

If you could see the plot, you might give it away. You might tell all of your friends "It's all a sham. There is no world, no heaven, no birth, no death, no self, no other, no ego, no God, no nothing." Can you imagine how embarrassing that would be for the powers that be? Even my job would be threatened. I might have to take early retirement!

Not that I wouldn't do it. I'd be only too happy to step down, knowing you too were off the proverbial cross. It would be a great relief for all concerned.

But you can't do that yet. You are still the observer. You are still limited by what you see.

"Well, I'll just close my eyes," you say. But what would that accomplish? Your fear of looking isn't going to remove the objects in front of you. They will remain, even though you cease to see them. And if you pretend they are not there, as soon as you begin moving about you will crash into them.

Something much more radical is needed if you want to break through the limits of your perception. Something resembling a spiritual practice perhaps.

Try this one: "What I see is a mirror showing me what I believe. Everything that happens in my life is a reflection of some belief I have about myself."

Try saying this to yourself, every time you start to take your life or someone else's life too seriously. Say it when you are in pain and feel you can't take another step forward. Say it when you are in love and can't wait another moment for your lover.

Open your eyes as you embrace the experience. Don't go to sleep. Don't pretend that you know what something means. Just remember that everything that happens is a reflection of a belief that you have. Just look without judging. Look in simple acceptance. Look in surrender.

You are the observer, but you too are being observed. You too are being watched, right now.

Who is the one watching?

I assure you it's not Big Brother.

It is like a rock skipping over the surface of the pond. You see it skipping, but you don't know who threw it.

You see the ripples, but you don't know who caused them.

204

Who is the one watching? Who are you?

Are you the observer or the observed, or both?

If no one hears the tree falling in the forest, does it make a sound?

What is the sound of one hand clapping?

Remember, you aren't going to figure any of this out, so just be present to it and throw all your interpretations out. Let go of your dogma and your isms. The only ism you need is the one you are, and in time that too will go. All borrowed identity will be dislodged. Only the naked being will remain: Adam, standing alone in the garden, face to face with God.

Divining

You can't help wanting to know the outcome. It is the nature of the ego to want to be prepared to meet experience. It feels safer in knowing.

However, it is not always safer. Sometimes knowing things in advance causes more fear.

Imagine for example that you are going to manifest cancer at age 50. You are 40 now. Would you want to know? Would it help you to know?

Knowing something like this can make you go into fear. Do you want to live for ten years in fear or would you prefer to confront the moment when it comes?

Of course, this is not a fair example. Rarely would it be possible for you to know what is going to happen ten years in advance. The events in your life are not predestined. Events are created out of experience, out of the dialogue between your beliefs and the possibilities that surround you. Different choices will lead to different outcomes.

Not only can't you know what is going to happen to you, but you can't know what meaning it will have to you. If you experience cancer as a wake up call to get your life on track, it will have a different meaning than if you experience it as a life sentence. How you react to what happens (the inner experience) is as crucial as what happens itself (the outer experience) in describing any event.

Since all perception of meaning is subjective, people react to similar external circumstances in very different ways. That is why you can never predict what anything will mean to another person. The event that one person responds to with compassion will stir up anger or resentment in another.

Understanding the subjective nature of experience is crucial to spiritual insight. People cannot control what happens to them in the present as a result of unconscious choices made in the past. Each person lives in the karmic flow of his life and while certain experiences may be perfect for the evolution of the soul, they are not necessarily consciously understood or appreciated.

The spiritual person learns increasingly to surrender to her experience. When events arise which seem to attack her, she listens within for the message hidden behind the veil of her subjective reactions. She works to see the soul value and potential for learning in each encounter. Her effort is not focused on trying to manipulate her experience to achieve the outcomes desired by her ego, but rather to commune with her experience to learn in the most profound way the lessons that it brings.

Her life is a dialogue between inner and outer, between what she sees and how she feels about it, between experience and her interpretation of it. Increasingly, she learns that her suffering is not caused by what happens, but by her subjective reaction to it. She is crucified not by someone else or some external event, but by the meaning she gives to what happens.

The hardest thing on earth is to see the attack of others as a call for love and support. One can do this only if one focuses not on the actions of the attacker, but on one's own response to those actions. In investigating one's own fear or anger, one becomes sensitive to the situation at hand. Looking within, and then looking without, one sees how fear invokes anger and anger invokes fear. One appreciates one's role as a participant in the larger human drama. Seeing oneself in the other and the other in oneself, compassion takes root in the heart and extends subtly to the other person.

The spiritual person does not look for someone to scapegoat or blame. He does not seek to make someone else responsible for his experience. He does not blame God for punishing him.

His commitment to the spiritual path begins with establishing a truce with God. He agrees not to hold God solely accountable for his experience. He agrees to share the accountability with God. He knows that his response to what happens determines its ultimate meaning, so that he and God are in dialogue about everything that occurs in his life.

That means that sometimes he is grateful to God and sometimes he gets mad at God. That's part of his dialogue with the divine.

There is always a portion of his experience which he finds unacceptable. There is always something he is in resistance to. There is always some aspect of experience where he looks without and cannot look within, some place where he can't be accountable, where he can't accept responsibility. And that place represents the cutting edge of spiritual growth in his life.

No matter how confused, resistant, and angry at God he may be, he remains in dialogue. He continues to find ways to look deeper and to come to greater acceptance of his life.

Gradually, he steps into the moment. He learns to be fully present. Even if being present means being angry or sad. He steps into the experience without apology.

He steps into the experience even if he does not know what it means or how he feels about it. He steps into the moment and tells the truth as he perceives it. And he knows that this is just the truth for this one moment. It may not be the truth for the next moment.

He knows that God asks only one thing from him and that is his willingness to be present, his willingness to be in dialogue. God is not afraid of his anger or his grief. She would not take these away from him. She does not ask that he behave in a particular way. She just asks him to hang in there, to be willing to learn.

The biggest obstruction in the relationship with God is the belief that you know. That belief makes you a prisoner of your own subjective interpretation. What you know is just your fear asserting itself.

Your description of reality is not reality. Your need to limit reality to fit your fear-based beliefs about it does not constitute "knowing." What you call knowing is just bias, prejudice, judgment.

When your judgments parade as the truth, you deceive everyone, including yourself. You close the channel to the divine. You shut God out. "Shut up, God," you say. "I know what I'm doing here."

Fortunately, God is patient, compassionate, and gifted with a great sense of humor. So His response is: "I'm sorry, sir, I did not realize you were the chess champion of the cosmos. I sincerely beg your pardon and gladly withdraw until you desire my presence."

A little sarcastic, perhaps, but to the point. God will never go up against your pride, nor will he punish you for it, contrary to popular notions to the contrary. In the face of your pride, God merely gets out of your way and waits for you to come to your senses.

Since every project you undertake without Him is doomed to failure, He rarely has to wait long before you're back knocking on the door. He knows that. That is why He is so patient and good humored about your fickleness and infidelity.

When the parent understands the child's mistakes without taking them personally, the parent can be patient and kind. It is only when the parent feels unworthy, judged or attacked that he intervenes inhospitably in the child's learning experience.

Fortunately, God does not feel unworthy and knows that he cannot be attacked. This we all have to learn from Him. Until we learn this we cannot take our place at His side.

The desire to know what we do not know is essential to the spiritual path. But spiritual knowledge is a different kind of knowledge than we are used to. It is not a knowledge that enables us to control and manipulate our lives or those of others. It does not enable us to predict events or interpret what they mean. It is a knowledge that enables us to look within, to see through the veil of our subjective reactions, to learn to appreciate the essence of life as it unfolds without attaching our own meaning to it.

Spiritual knowledge comes from giving up what we think we know and surrendering to what is. It is more an unknowing than an knowing, more an emptying than a taking in.

Spiritual knowing is not a left brained phenomena. It does not rationalize or interpret. It is not systematic or causal. It does not separate content from form or inner from outer.

Many people have tried to divine with left brain systems and they invariably come up empty. All the intellectual systems — the tarots, kabbalahs, numerologies, astrologies, etc. — are self-limited and limiting. They cater to your ego's illusion of understanding and foster spiritual pride.

Used for divination — for guidance in the moment — symbolical systems can be helpful. But one moment's guidance is not necessarily relevant to the demands of the next. To attempt to "freeze" reality, which is dynamic and always changing, to fit an external reference point is to lose touch with the flow of spontaneity and grace.

The desire to figure things out before they happen is one of the ego's defenses against the truth. This defense must be surrendered before the truth can be placed in your hands.

Prayer

Prayer is the ongoing dialogue with God. It is the process by which one continually empties out what one thinks one knows and surrenders to the mystery in the moment.

Prayer is not petitioning God for certain outcomes or results. Petitioning is exactly what it sounds like. How do you feel when you are petitioned? How would you expect God to feel?

A nagging child never wins his parents honest attention or good will. Why approach God as a nagging child? It is neither dignified nor effective.

If you want your prayers to be effective, approach God as a loving parent, as Father or Mother. Tell Him or Her what you are thinking and feeling. Admit your fears and your judgments and ask that you be strengthened to walk through them. Ask to see beyond your preconceptions and prejudices and to open to the truth. Ask to learn the lesson the situation brings. Ask for guidance, support, help, relief from suffering. Ask for the highest good of all concerned.

And then be quiet and abide with Him. Let your mind be joined with His mind. Let your heart open to His love. Let understanding come organically as heart and mind open to a greater reality than the one you have yet been able to perceive.

Your divine parents have the answer to your dilemma. You need but open to them and the solution will emerge in your heart.

And you will know that it is the solution because it honors everyone, because it resolves your internal conflict. You will know it is the answer because your heart will be uplifted. Energy and optimism will return to your life. You will breathe more freely. You will look forward to the unfolding of reality.

Guidance like this is available to you whenever you pray in earnest, whenever you open your heart to God and listen to Her answer. Prayer is your gesture of opening, confiding, asking for help. Guidance is Her response. It brings comfort, clarity, and peace to you.

If you already know what the answer is or "should be," then you can't really pray. Prayer comes from the place of not knowing.

Whenever you pray and your prayers are not answered, it is either because you made a demand or because you did not surrender mentally or emotionally. You held onto your wound or your opinions, instead of giving them to God. Or you rejected God's answer because it did not conform to your expectations.

If you seek validation of your ego perceptions through prayer, you will be disappointed. If you ask God, He will tell you the truth. He won't tell you what you want to hear.

Successful prayer always takes you into a spiritual state in which your heart and mind are more open than they were before. It always helps you to see things differently, more generously, more expansively. It never agrees with your narrowness, your judgments, or justifies your need to attack or defend.

Prayer is an opening on your part to receive the gifts of God. It is an opening to God's unconditional love for you. It is an opening to God's unconditional acceptance of you as you are.

When you enter the temple of prayer, you are blessed beyond measure. You cannot emerge from the temple bearing ill feelings toward others or toward yourself. For, in entering, you surrender, and, in surrendering, you are washed clean of all judgments you make about yourself or others.

Can you pray? That is a good question!

Are you willing to surrender what you think you know? Are you willing to allow for the possibility that there may be a more transcendent way of perceiving your life situation?

If not, then be with the truth of that. Don't force yourself to pray. Wait until you are ready. Then your prayer will have integrity. Then you will open to God's wisdom and grace.

Spiritual Work

The most profound learning you do happens when you find yourself reacting strongly to what someone else says or does. While the tendency in this situation is to focus on the other person's behavior, the truth is that your reaction has nothing to do with the other person. Your reaction shows where you are in conflict, not where the other person is.

All conflict comes from some kind of guilt or insecurity you are feeling. If you are feeling insecure about your intelligence and someone comes along and calls you stupid, your buttons get pushed. The reaction comes from your insecurity. The trigger is incidental. Anyone could push your buttons.

If you are sleeping with someone who is married and you feel guilty about it, you are going to react when someone calls you a betrayer. Your reaction is based on the fact that you have the perception of yourself as a betrayer and the other person just triggers it. If you did not see yourself as a betrayer, you would not react defensively to the comment.

The need to defend yourself comes from a perception of guilt on your part. When attacked or insulted by another, you become hurt and/or angry only when you think there is some justification for the attack. You feel that you have done something wrong and now you have been found out. You know you deserve to be punished, so the only thing you can do to avoid punishment is to defend yourself.

Defense is admission of guilt. Why would you defend if you did not feel guilty? You would merely laugh and say "Nice try, brother."

You would not take the attack personally. You would see that the person is just attacking himself and you were the trigger. You would know that it is not your fault that he or she is in pain.

Every fear or insecurity you have about yourself is a button waiting to be pushed. The fact that people push

212

these buttons is not at all remarkable. What is remarkable is that you blame them for pushing them.

When you wear a sign that says "hit me," are you surprised that a few people come along and take you literally? True, not everyone does. Some people just laugh and move along. But others stop and glare at you or take you at your word. They are wearing a sign that says"hit me" too. They know how you feel. They know that you need to be hit to feel better about yourself. You have been a bad girl or boy and you need to be punished. They are only too happy to oblige.

People who attack you are doing what they, in their self-deluded way, think you want them to do. They are doing it "for your own good."   They are always able to justify their behavior toward you and you in turn can justify it too.

Never do you think "this is unacceptable. This should not and cannot happen. I will not permit it. " If the abused were to believe and communicate this fully, abuse could not happen. Abuse happens in the grey space of guilt and punishment.

All you have to do to stop trespass in your life is to say: "This does not feel good. Will you please stop?" Such a simple request, yet it is phenomenally hard for you to make it. Why?

Many reasons. Perhaps you are a child being abused by an adult. The adult is the authority figure. Often it is a parent whom you love. Even if you are an adult, the same patterns operate. You want the abuser's love and approval, regardless of the costs to you, so you minimize the pain, or dissociate from it totally. Or you accept that you deserve the pain because you are unworthy.

Adults who are victimized seek to recreate the pain of childhood trauma so that they can break through patterns of dissociation, recall the abuse and come to conscious grips with the wounds. That is why they frequently marry a person who is exactly like their abuser. Only by aggravating the wound can the shell of unconscious denial be cracked. The release of suppressed rage, guilt and self-hatred open the door to healing and integration.

There   are   many   versions   of   self-betrayal.

Understanding your version is important.

Blaming your abuser will not free you from the cycle of violence, because the pattern is a self-generating one, albeit at an unconscious level. As long as you stay in victimhood and blame, you will carry the pattern forward, passing the wound on from generation to generation. And all because you do not have the courage to look within.

By making the pattern conscious, you can fully experience the self-violation, forgive yourself, and make a conscious decision to be a victim no longer. That and that alone stops the cycle of self-betrayal.

Regardless of which path into pain you have chosen — and there are so many — you will stay in pain until you turn to your abuser and say: "This is unacceptable to me. I want you to stop right now." You must say this without any reservation. You must clearly let the other person know: "I would rather lose your love than let this trespass continue."

You must stand up for yourself.

Until you have the courage to stand up fully inside your life, someone will always be around to abuse you. Indeed, you will keep calling abusers to you till you until you decide that you have had enough. So every time your buttons get pushed, recognize that it is a gift to you, a chance to become conscious of your pattern of self-betrayal. Don't blame the abuser. Instead ask yourself "Why did I allow myself to once again to be drawn into a situation in which I am not respected and listened to?" Become conscious of the fear and self-judgment that are running your life. See your low self image. See how you accept love at any price. See how you keep recycling your fear of abandonment because you are afraid to face it head on.

Stop the game of reacting to others. Refuse to be an object, even though being an object seems to offer you what you want. Look at your experience so far and learn from it. Promises of conditional love have given you nothing. Their unfulfillment has just deepened your feelings of being betrayed and abandoned by those you love.

Remind yourself that you decided to play the object game. You gave permission. Acknowledge your mistake, your self-violation, so that you won't repeat it. Take responsibility. Stop projecting blame. Let the lie go. No one is a victim unless he decides to be one.

Regardless of what you believe about what happened in the past, recognize that you cannot go on with your life without learning to say no to abuse here and now. Don't make this a philosophical or moral issue. Learn to say no to invitations to self-betrayal right now.

Like an alcoholic who can't say no to alcohol, you can't say no to the conditional promise of love. Admit your powerlessness. You cannot overcome your unconscious pattern of self-betrayal without help. And the help you need is conscious awareness. You need to see how you go unconscious, how you give yourself up to abuse, again and again.

Until you see the pattern and take responsibility for breaking it, it will continue. It doesn't matter how much therapy you have or how many treatment programs you have been in.

The alcoholic declines the drink because he sees that taking it means giving up his power. You decline to be an object of abuse for the same reason.

You see, as long as you perceive the problem outside of you, you won't solve it. You will blame others, blame the institutions of society, blame God, but the problem will remain. Because the problem is self-betrayal. Until you learn to say yes to yourself, you won't be able to say no to others.

The problem is never that "others" betray you. Others merely mirror back to you your our own beliefs about yourself.

Others give you the gift of self-reflection. Without the help of others in reflecting back to you your unconscious assumptions, your awakening process would take considerably longer.

Your brother is your teacher.. He shows you what you need to look at in yourself. And you do the same for him.

This is the drama of awakening.

Do not make it a soap opera. Do not make your brother or sister responsible for your experience. They can never be responsible for your experience.

Your fellow human beings are not meant to be either scapegoats or demigods. They are not the cause of your suffering, nor are they the cause of your salvation.

They are equal passengers on the same journey. What you have felt, they have also felt. Like you, they are learning to see their own patterns of self betrayal. Like you, they are learning to say yes to self and no to giving their power away.

Be patient. This is a journey to full empowerment. When the self is empowered fully, abuse will be impossible.

Awakening Together

When two people commit to a spiritual relationship, they agree to help each other become conscious of the patterns of self-betrayal. Their intention is not to stuff their negative feelings, but to create enough safety in their relationship that negative feelings can surface and the patterns of self-betrayal can be revealed.

Spiritual companionship involves not only sharing a common purpose and orientation toward life, it also involves a mutual, courageous commitment to take responsibility and undo blame. Each person is here to help his partner stop projecting, stop playing the victim, stop finding problems outside herself. He does this not by lecturing her, but by creating a safe, compassionate space where she may come face to face with herself.

Where she would see an enemy, he cannot join her. He refuses to join the game of scapegoating, blame or attack. But he can love. He can accept how she feels. He can validate her feelings and encourage her gently to find the path to peace within her own heart.

Although he sees her go into projection, he does not try to fix her, because that would mean joining her in the lie. He simply stays conscious of who she really is. And so he calls her gently, non-verbally, back to herself.

Most of all, he just listens. He doesn't agree or disagree with what she has to say. He knows his opinion means nothing and, if anything, will take her away from her process. He just listens deeply and compassionately. He listens without judgment or, if he finds himself judging, he becomes aware of his own judgments and brings himself back to listening. He listens with an open heart and an open mind. And his listening becomes a grounding rod to truth. The more he listens to her without judgment, the more her journey of blame slows down. Gradually, using the pathway of his love, she returns to herself.

This is the gift the spiritual partner provides to his or her mate. This is the pearl of great price.

When each can give the other the gift of unconditional acceptance and love, extending that gift to include everyone, there will be no more projection, no more blame, no more attack. There will be no more objects. No more victims or abusers.

There will be equal partners in the dance of life. There will be the heart opening. A little at first, but then so wide, it threatens to swallow the whole manifest universe. And indeed, one day it will.

When all that perceives itself as unworthy and unwhole becomes whole and holy, there will be no more perceived separation from the source of love. Each of us will be a radiant beam of light from the center of the heart, reaching out throughout all eternity, dissolving separation and sin, baptizing the guilty in the river of their own fear, and greeting them with bouquets of flowers as they emerge from the waters, innocent and free.

These are the gifts we have to offer each other when the game of abuse is over. And it is over in any moment in which we remember who we are and who our sister truly is.

Namaste

Namaste. I accept your humanness and mine. And I also bow to the divinity in each of us. I accept our absolute spiritual equality as beings. And I also accept that we each forget who we are.

I celebrate the fact that we are waking up together, and I appreciate the fact that, as each of us pushes up against our fear, we nod off to sleep.

I acknowledge both the absolute and the relative, for both are present here. The gentle voice of God and the passionate cries of the wounded child commingle here, in this mind, in this world. Joy and sadness commingle. Strength and tears, beauty and betrayal, silence and cacophony interpenetrate.

It is a simple world, breathing in and breathing out, approaching the divine and moving away. And it is also complex in its near infinite variety of forms.

Each self is the unqualified presence, yet each must approach God in its own unique way. Within oneness, paradox abounds.

Here we dwell together, my brother and sister.

Here in the silence, each of us with our unique heartbeat, our own dance, our own call for love and truth.

Yet despite the division into bodies, despite the fragmentation of the mind, only one heart opens here. And that heart includes yours and mine and that of all beings who have ever lived in time and space. That heart belongs to God. His patient heart. Her infinite blessing on us all. My wish for you is a simple one. May you find that Heart in your heart. May you find your voice in that silence. May you awaken to the truth of who you are.

Namaste!

Paul Ferrini is the author of numerous books which help us heal the emotional body and embrace a spirituality grounded in the real challenges of daily life. Paul's work is heart-centered and experiential, empowering us to move through our fear and shame and share who we are authentically with others. Paul Ferrini is the editor of *Miracles Magazine*, a publication devoted to telling Miracle Stories that offer hope and inspiration to all of us. Paul's conferences, retreats and *Affinity Group Process* have helped thousands of people deepen their practice of forgiveness and open their hearts to the Divine presence in themselves and others. For more information on *Miracles Magazine,* workshops, retreats or *The Affinity Group Process*, contact *The Miracles Community Network*, P.O. Box 181, South Deerfield, MA 01373 or call 413-665-0555.

Heartways Press

"Integrating Spirituality into Daily Life"
Books by Paul Ferrini

• **Love Without Conditions:
Reflections of the Christ Mind**

An incredible book from Jesus calling us to awaken to our own Christhood. Rarely has any book conveyed the teachings of the master in such a simple but profound manner. This book will help you to bring your understanding from the head to the heart so that you can model the teachings of love and forgiveness in your daily life.192 pp. paper ISBN 1-879159-15-5 $12.00

• **The Wisdom of the Self**

This ground-breaking book explores our authentic experience and our journey to wholeness. "Your life is your spiritual path. Don't be quick to abandon it for promises of bigger and better experiences. You are getting exactly the experiences you need to grow. If your growth seems too slow or uneventful for you, it is because you have not fully embraced the situations and relationships at hand ... To know the Self is to allow everything, to embrace the totality of who we are, all that we think and feel, all of our fear, all of our love." 229 pp. paper ISBN 1-879159-14-7 $12.00

• **The Twelve Steps Of Forgiveness**

A practical manual for healing ourselves and our relationships. This book gives us a step by step process for moving through our fears, projections, judgments, and guilt so that we can take responsibility for creating the life we want. With great gentleness, we learn to embrace our lessons and to find equality with others. A must read for all in recovery and others seeking spiritual wholeness. 128 pp. paper ISBN 1-879159-10-4 $10.00

• The Circle of Atonement

This book explores a healing process in which we confront our deep-seated guilt and fear, bringing love and forgiveness to the wounded child within. By surrendering our judgments of self and others, we overcome feelings of separation and dismantle co-dependent patterns that restrict our self-expression and ability to give and receive love. 224 pp. paper ISBN 1-879159-06-6 $12.00

• The Bridge to Reality

A Heart-centered Approach to *A Course in Miracles* and the Process of Inner Healing. Sharing his experiences of spiritual awakening, Paul emphasizes self-acceptance and forgiveness as cornerstones of spiritual practice. Presented with beautiful photos, this book conveys the essence of *The Course* as it is lived in daily life. 192 pp. paper ISBN 1-879159-03-1 $12.00

• From Ego To Self

108 illustrated affirmations designed to offer you a new way of viewing conflict situations so that you can overcome negative thinking and bring more energy, faith and optimism into your life. 128 pp. paper ISBN 1-879159-01-5 $10.00

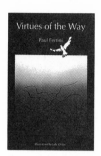

• Virtues Of The Way
A lyrical work of contemporary scripture reminiscent of the Tao Te Ching. Beautifully illustrated, this inspirational book will help you cultivate the spiritual values required to fulfill your creative purpose and live in harmony with others. 64 pp. paper ISBN 1-879159-02-3 $7.50

• The Body Of Truth
A crystal clear introduction to the universal teachings of love and forgiveness. This book traces all forms of suffering to negative attitudes and false beliefs, which we have the ability to transform. 64 pp. paper ISBN 1-879159-02-3 $7.50

• Available Light
Inspirational, passionate poems dealing with the work of inner integration, love and relationships, death and re-birth, loss and abundance, life purpose and the reality of spiritual vision.   128 pp. paper   ISBN 1-879159-05-8 $12.00

Guided Meditation Cassette Tapes
by Paul Ferrini

• The Circle of Healing
It's finally available. The meditation and healing tape that many of you have been requesting for months is now here. This gentle meditation opens the heart to love's presence and extends that love to all the beings in your experience. A powerful tape with inspirational piano accompaniment by Michael Gray.
ISBN #1-879159-08-2 $10.00

• Healing the Wounded Child
A potent healing tape that accesses old feelings of pain, fragmentation, self-judgment and separation and brings them into the light of conscious awareness and acceptance. Side two includes hauntingly beautiful "inner child" reading from The Bridge to Reality with piano accompaniment by Michael Gray.
ISBN #1-879159-11-2 $10.00

• Forgiveness: Returning to the Original Blessing
A Self Healing tape that helps us accept and learn from the mistakes we have made in the past. By letting go of our judgments and ending our ego-based search for perfection, we can bring our darkness to the light, dissolving anger, guilt, and shame. Piano accompaniment by Michael Gray.
ISBN #1-879159-12-0 $10.00

Heartways Press
Order Form

Name_____

Address_____

City _____State _____Zip _____

Phone _____

BOOKS

The Silence of the Heart ($14.95)   _____

Love Without Conditions ($12.00)   _____

The Wisdom of the Self ($12.00)   _____

The Twelve Steps of Forgiveness ($10.00) _____

The Circle of Atonement ($12.00)   _____

The Bridge of Reality ($12.00)   _____

From Ego to Self ($10.00)   _____

Virtues of the Way ($7.50)   _____

The Body of Truth ($7.50)   _____

Available Light ($10.00)   _____

TAPES

The Circle of Healing ($10.00)   _____

Healing the Wounded Child ($10.00)   _____

Forgiveness: Returning to the Original Blessing ($10.00) _____

SHIPPING

($2.00 for first item, $.50 each additional item.

Add additional $1.00 for first class postage.)   _____

MA residents please add 5% sales tax.   _____

TOTAL $_____

Send Order To: Heartways Press
P. O. Box 181
South Deerfield, MA 01373
Tel: 413-665-0555

Please allow 1-2 weeks for delivery